HOCKEY
PLAY-BY-PLAY

Around the NHL with Jim Robson

HOCKEY
PLAY-BY-PLAY

Around the NHL with Jim Robson

JASON FARRIS

with editorial contributions by John Shorthouse
layout by Adrienne Painter

circaNOW!
PRODUCTIONS

Library and Archives Canada Cataloguing in Publication

Farris, Jason, 1967-
    Hockey play-by-play : around the NHL with Jim Robson
/ Jason Farris ; with editorial contributions by John
Shorthouse ; layout by Adrienne Painter.

ISBN 0-9739016-1-6

    1. National Hockey League--History. 2. Vancouver
Canucks (Hockey team)--History. 3. Robson, Jim, 1935-.
 4. Hockey--Canada--History. 5. Hockey--United States--
History. 6. Sportscasters--British Columbia--Vancouver.
I. Shorthouse, John II. Robson, Jim, 1935- III. Title.

GV847.8.N3F37 2005   796.962'64'09   C2005-905360-7

Editor: Lloyd Davis
Proofreader: Neall Calvert
Art Direction: Jason Farris
Book design: Adrienne Painter
Cover design: Rebecca Davies

First printing October 2005
Printed in Hong Kong

circaNow Productions
a division of Janex Holdings Inc.
1437 Kings Avenue
West Vancouver, B.C., Canada V7T 2C7
Tel: (604) 803-4561 *Fax:* (604) 922-1488
www.robsonhockeybook.com

**For trade sales and distribution in
Canada and the United States contact:**

The News Group
Attention: Book Re-Order Department
2500 Vauxhall Place
Richmond, BC
Canada V6V 1Y8
Tel: 1-800-667-4764 extension 145
Fax: 1-800-336-1633
Email: breorders@van.thenewsgroup.com

Part proceeds go to
Canuck Place
Children's Hospice.
www.canuckplace.org

Hockey Play-by-Play is also available in
a hardcover version –a limited edition
of 1000 numbered copies signed by
Jim Robson and John Shorthouse

Author Dedication

T his book is dedicated to all the guys on the 1984–85 Clams, Breezeways, Chiefs and No-Names — and their innumerable variants from our preceding dozen years of after-school road hockey. Those endless hours of enjoyment with great friends were often filled with big-league dreams and were always accompanied by imitations of Jim Robson's play-by-play. In particular, this book is dedicated to Brian MacKenzie, Hugh Meikle and Jim Wall, lifelong friends with whom I've enjoyed countless hours listening to the real Jim Robson broadcasts. I trust that this book remains true to the game of hockey as we love and remember it from our boyhoods. I hope the three of you will have fun sharing our memories, and this book, with your kids, nieces and nephews.

The Pregame Show
with John Shorthouse

Like a lot of kids growing up in Vancouver in the 1970s and '80s, I developed an early and intense love affair with the Canucks. I still have vivid memories of my first game—January 24, 1976, just a week before my sixth birthday—when I watched Vancouver battle the Toronto Maple Leafs to a 5–5 tie. It was my first trip to the Pacific Coliseum that didn't involve seeing the circus.

Three memories stand out clear as day. First, there was the hilarious fake moustache my brother Tom doodled onto Babe Pratt's face in one of the advertisements in the program. Second, the sickening thud of a puck slamming full force into the stomach of Harold Snepts as he went down fearlessly to block a lethal slap shot. It's a sound I've yet to hear duplicated, but one that resonated so clearly, even up in the "greens." My final memory is this: I remember that the game didn't seem nearly as exciting or interesting without Jim Robson there.

You see, like many Lower Mainlanders, I had yet to realize the truth: that as much as I loved hockey, and as much as I loved the Canucks, my real love affair was with that voice that piped through the airwaves and kept me abreast of all the goings-on of my favourite team.

My birthday was the next week, and I was delighted to unwrap the portable transistor radio that had quickly shot up to the top of my wish list. It would accompany me to the "Rink on Renfrew" on countless occasions over the years.

Growing up a Canucks fan wasn't exactly the easiest thing in the world. There were a few bright spots in the team's first couple of decades, but more often than not the franchise was closer to being a punchline than a powerhouse.

From the original spin of the wheel that saw Gilbert Perreault become Buffalo Sabre, to the hideous uniforms of the '80s that only a mother (or a fan of the San Diego Padres) could love, cheering for the home team brought with it an

Above: Jim shares a laugh with Canucks coach Phil Maloney during the 1975–76 season, his last as an NHL coach.

Right: John donning the pads for "Honest Nat's" Department store (♪"48th & Fraser") in Vancouver circa 1978.

Far right: Living out a boyhood dream: John shares a pre-game moment with Jim in the Jim Robson Broadcast Booth at GM Place.

inordinate amount of razzing from fans of the more established and more successful NHL entries.

And then there was the on-ice product.

In nineteen of their first twenty-one seasons, the Canucks finished with more losses than wins. Included in that was an incredible run of fifteen consecutive sub-.500 seasons, from 1976–77 to 1990–91.

And yet, through all the tough times, we as followers of the Vancouver Canucks could always lay claim to one consistent source of pride: we had absolutely the best play-by-play announcer in the entire league, and arguably in the history of the NHL.

The distinctive sound of Hall of Fame broadcaster Jim Robson was our conduit to the world of hockey. His eyes and voice took us to mysterious places like the Cap Center in Landover, Maryland; the Kemper Arena in Kansas City, Missouri; the Omni in Atlanta, Georgia; and the Civic Center Coliseum in Hartford, Connecticut.

To a youngster who had decided early on that he wanted to become the play-by-play voice of the Vancouver Canucks, these less-celebrated destinations held as much allure as Maple Leaf Gardens, Chicago Stadium, Joe Louis Arena or the Forum in Montreal.

Eventually, of course, I would get the chance to visit many of these places. But for most hockey fans, Jim's broadcasts were as close as they'd ever got to experiencing a game in another NHL city.

That's why we hope you'll enjoy *Hockey Play-by-Play.*

Armed with a pair of game tickets, a program and Jim's handwritten notes, you'll get the chance to relive more than thirty great road games from the 1970s, '80s and '90s.

For each game you'll get a feel for the hockey pulse of the home cities, the subtleties of their rinks, what went on in the broadcast booth and, of course, memories of some of Jim's great play-by-play calls.

And while games involving the Canucks will dominate these pages, there are others that will cause you to reminisce as well. The "Fog Game" in Buffalo in 1975, and the Bob Nystrom goal that won the 1980 Stanley Cup for the Islanders are just two of the many highlights of Jim Robson's illustrious career.

Understandably, there are cities and rinks that Jim is unfamiliar with in this ever-evolving NHL. To that end, I've been asked to play a small role in this book as well, and for that I'm grateful to both Jim and the author. I'll take you to the nine newest NHL cities and profile a memorable night in each, featuring your current Canucks heroes: Jovanovski, Naslund, Cloutier, Linden and others.

To paraphrase Jim's familiar midgame refrain to "shut-ins," this book is for the fans who couldn't get out to the road games around the NHL, but love the league and want to experience game day in each NHL city.

We hope it's an experience you'll remember.

PERIOD 1 2 3 OT

The Lineup

PERIOD 1 2 3 OT

The Pregame Warmup
Guide to Reading Jim Robson's Game Notes

Abbreviations:

St. Gl — *Starting Goalies—circled number represent shutouts to date.*

NDr — *Not Dressed. "—H" indicates a player is hurt; all others are usually considered healthy scratches.*

Op — *Operator; also referred to as the technical or broadcast engineer.*

Ref — *Referee.*

LM — *Linesmen. In playoff games, "SB" indicates standby officials.*

INT — *Intermission features. Usually lists which guest was interviewed on the broadcast and who conducted the interview. Most-common interviewers included AD—Al Davidson, JR—Jim Robson, TL—Tom Larscheid, GM—Garry Monahan, JP—J. Paul McConnell.*

SOG — *Shots on goal. Period totals for both teams are noted; cumulative game totals for both teams are circled.*

Prev — *Previous records or game results (R—Road, H—Home)*

PP — *PowerPlay*
PK — *Penalty Killing*
SHG — *Shorthanded Goals*
GAA — *Goals Against Average*
GF — *Goals For*
OT — *Overtime*
SO — *Shutouts*

L'LAND — *Lumberland—Local sponsor that contributed to the CKNW Orphans' Fund for every Canuck goal.*

SHUT-INS — *Jim's reminder to himself to mention his familiar refrain (usually mentioned during the middle of the 2nd period) welcoming "shut-ins, pensioners, the blind and those fans that cannot get out to the games…"*

✗ ✔ — *Cross-checking*
ENG — *Empty Net Goal*
Atnd — *Attendance (SO—Sell out)*
RAM — *Canuck player selected as the Dodge "RAM Tough" award winner*

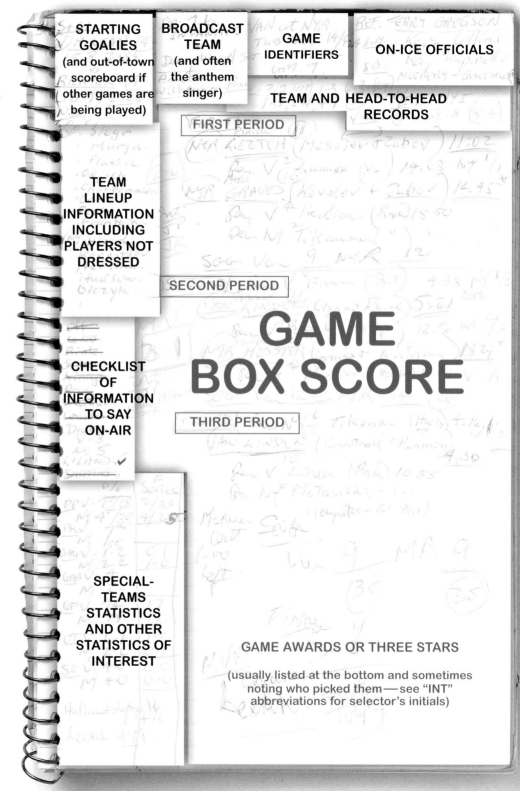

STARTING GOALIES (and out-of-town scoreboard if other games are being played)

BROADCAST TEAM (and often the anthem singer)

GAME IDENTIFIERS

ON-ICE OFFICIALS

TEAM AND HEAD-TO-HEAD RECORDS

FIRST PERIOD

TEAM LINEUP INFORMATION INCLUDING PLAYERS NOT DRESSED

SECOND PERIOD

CHECKLIST OF INFORMATION TO SAY ON-AIR

GAME BOX SCORE

THIRD PERIOD

SPECIAL-TEAMS STATISTICS AND OTHER STATISTICS OF INTEREST

GAME AWARDS OR THREE STARS

(usually listed at the bottom and sometimes noting who picked them—see "INT" abbreviations for selector's initials)

2

| PREPARED BEFORE THE GAME | RECORDED DURING THE GAME |

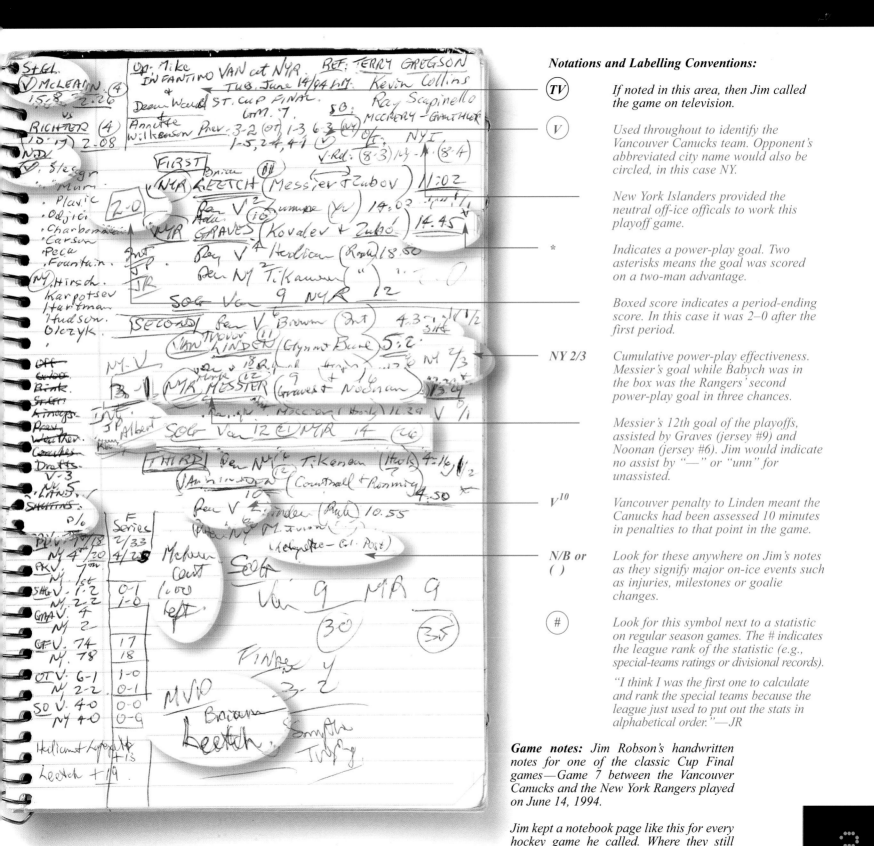

Notations and Labelling Conventions:

TV — If noted in this area, then Jim called the game on television.

V — Used throughout to identify the Vancouver Canucks team. Opponent's abbreviated city name would also be circled, in this case NY.

New York Islanders provided the neutral off-ice officals to work this playoff game.

* — Indicates a power-play goal. Two asterisks means the goal was scored on a two-man advantage.

Boxed score indicates a period-ending score. In this case it was 2–0 after the first period.

NY 2/3 — Cumulative power-play effectiveness. Messier's goal while Babych was in the box was the Rangers' second power-play goal in three chances.

V¹⁰ — Messier's 12th goal of the playoffs, assisted by Graves (jersey #9) and Noonan (jersey #6). Jim would indicate no assist by "—" or "unn" for unassisted.

Vancouver penalty to Linden meant the Canucks had been assessed 10 minutes in penalties to that point in the game.

N/B or ( ) — Look for these anywhere on Jim's notes as they signify major on-ice events such as injuries, milestones or goalie changes.

— Look for this symbol next to a statistic on regular season games. The # indicates the league rank of the statistic (e.g., special-teams ratings or divisional records).

"I think I was the first one to calculate and rank the special teams because the league just used to put out the stats in alphabetical order."—JR

Game notes: *Jim Robson's handwritten notes for one of the classic Cup Final games—Game 7 between the Vancouver Canucks and the New York Rangers played on June 14, 1994.*

Jim kept a notebook page like this for every hockey game he called. Where they still exist, they have been reproduced for the memorable nights that follow.

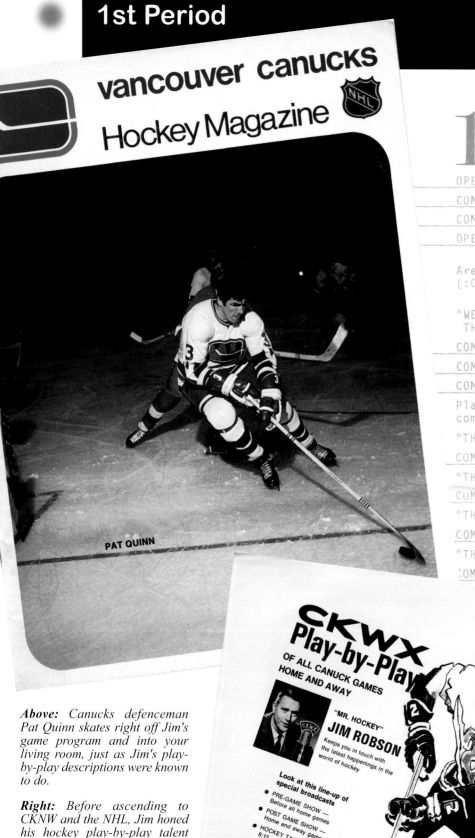

vancouver canucks
Hockey Magazine
NHL

PAT QUINN

1st pe

OPENING

COMMERCIAL - CLIENT

COMMERCIAL - CLIENT

OPENING CONTINUED

Arena starts 75 sec. aft
(:01:15) until one minut

"WE'LL RETURN FOR THE OP
THIS..."

COMMERCIAL - CLIENT

COMMERCIAL - CLIENT

COMMERCIAL - CLIENT

Play-by-play -- three 30
commercials inserted

"THE SCORE...THIS IS NHL

COMMERCIAL - CLIENT

"THE SCORE...MORE HOCKEY

COMMERCIAL - CLIENT

"THE SCORE....FROM   (ar

COMMERCIAL - CLIENT

"THE SCORE....MORE CANUC

COMMERCIAL - CLIENT

        CLIENT

    iod....

  ST PERIOD

  SUMMARY IN A MOMENT:"

   IENT   CART #

   IENT   CART #

  mment to:-

 R CANUCKS NHL HOCKEY IN THREE MINUTES"

   IENT   CART #

 S

   CLIENT   CART #

   CLIENT   CART #

Schedule of Memorable Nights

OCTOBER

			1	2	3	4	5
PIT/FLA 6 '76 / '00	7	8	DET 9 1995	BOS 10 1973	TOR 11 1970	12	
13	EDM 14 1979	15	16	17	18	19	
20	21	22	23	24	25	26	
TOR 27 1971	28	29	30	PHO 31 2003			

NOVEMBER

						1	2
3	4	5	6	7	EDM 8 1985	9	
10	QUE/MIN 11 '89 / '01	12	13	NJ 14 1996	15	16	
MIN 17 1989	18	19	20	21	DAL/ATL 22 '95 / '99	23	
STL 24 1990	NYR 25 1997	26	CAR 27 2002	28	29	30	

 HOME year   AWAY year

JIM ROBSON

" what a difference a voice makes"

Above: Canucks defenceman Pat Quinn skates right off Jim's game program and into your living room, just as Jim's play-by-play descriptions were known to do.

Right: Before ascending to CKNW and the NHL, Jim honed his hockey play-by-play talent calling Western League games on radio station CKWX.

Above: CKNW's hockey broadcast script showing commercial queues.

DECEMBER

	2	3	4	5	6	7
A 99	9	**TOR** 10 1980	11	12	13	14
16	17	18	19	20	21	
23	24	25	26	27	**SJ** 28 1991	
IL 72	30	31				

NUARY

		BOS 1 1973	2	3	**COL** 4 1980
	MTL 7 1987		9	10	11
13	14	15	**PROV** 16 ◄ 1968	17	18
SH 99	**WPG** 20 1984	21	22	23	**DET** 24 1971	25
27	28	29	30	31	

Western Hockey League

BRUARY

						1
	3	4	5	6	7	**All Star** 8 1983
	DET 10 1982	**BUF/TB** 12 '93 / '94	13	**WASH** 14 1978	15
OL 04	**CLEV** 17 1978	18	19	20	**BOS** 21 2000	22
3	24	25	26	27	28	

MARCH

			1
	OAK 3 <TML> 1970		
2	**HART** 3 1985	4	5	**KC/CBJ** 6 '76 / '03	7	8
9	10	11	12	**NYR** 13 1976	14	15
16	17	18	19	20	**ATL** 21 1975	22
LA 23 1994	24	25	26	27	28	29
30	31					

APRIL

		1	2	3	**OTT** 4 1993	5
6	7	8	9	**PHIL** 10 1979	11	12
13	**CAL** 14 1999	**MON** 15 1975	16	17	18	19
20	**CAL** 21 <EDM> 1988	22	23	24	25	26
27	28	**CHI** 29 1982	30			

<EDM> Edmonton at Calgary, "Battle of Alberta" classic

MAY

		1	2	3
4	5	6	7	**NYI** 8 1982	9	10
11	12	13	14	15	16	17
18	19	20	21	22	23	**NYI** 24 <PHIL> 1980
25	26	**BUF/CHI** 27 <PHIL> '75 / '95	28	29	30	31

<PHIL> Philadelphia at Buffalo Sabres, 1975

JUNE

1	2	3	4	5	6	7
8	9	10	**NYR** 11 1994	12	13	14
15	16	17	18	19	20	21
22	23	24	25	26	27	28
29	30					

HOCKEY PLAY-BY-PLAY
Around the NHL with Jim Robson

I'm proud of my handwritten records. I'm happy to show them to people so they can see how much effort I put into my broadcasts. Most guys didn't keep such detailed notes. Part of my reason for taking them stemmed from the fact that I worked alone in the early years. I didn't have access to a lot of statistics, so I kept my own. I used to keep game-by-game stats for each player. Now they are all available on the Internet.

Above: *Jim's Notes record that Bruin Chris Oddleifson (1G/1A) and Canuck Bobby Schmautz (0G/2A) both had strong nights. Later that season, they would be traded for each other. Their paths crossed again briefly in 1980–81 when they ended their careers as teammates in Vancouver.*

Facing bottom: *Ticket to the Blazers' 1975 team wind-up dinner, which ended up being the "franchise" wind-up dinner. They became the Calgary Cowboys for 1975–76.*

Bruins' League Leaders Blaze by Canucks
Vancouver Canucks @ Boston Bruins – October 10, 1973

On the first night of the 1973–74 season, the Canucks found themselves under attack on two fronts. On the road front, the Canucks faced off in Boston against the Big Bad Bruins. Meanwhile, back home, the loyalty of 12,452 Vancouver hockey fans was tested as the WHA's Vancouver Blazers played and won their inaugural game, 4–3 in overtime, against the Winnipeg Jets.

In time, the Canucks would become familiar with the likes of Blazers Jim Adair, Don Burgess, Danny Lawson and Claude St. Sauveur, but their immediate focus was on the more established threat posed by Phil Esposito, Ken Hodge, Wayne Cashman and Bobby Orr. Even Bruins coach Bep Guidolin gloated before the game, "Orr is really going great." In stark contrast to today's rigorous off-season conditioning programs, Guidolin went on to pronounce that Orr was in top shape because "he started playing tennis in August."

Vancouver did well to stay in the game with the more powerful Bruins — midway through the third they had battled back to tie the score, 4–4. But the Bruins just had too much firepower. Esposito netted a hat trick, including his 400th career goal, to go with two assists; Hodge had a goal and two helpers; Cashman a goal and an assist; and Orr, who "only" chipped in two assists, was on the ice for all six Boston goals.

The Canucks were not the only team to be victimized by this quartet of Boston snipers. By season's end, they held down the top four spots in the NHL scoring race. It was only the second time in league history that this had happened: the Bruins also turned the trick in 1970–71 (Espo, Orr, Hodge and John Bucyk). Dominant offence was a Boston tradition of sorts — the 1939–40 Bruins boasted four of the league's top five scorers.

The Canucks lost both the road and home battles on this night. But within two seasons they would win the war for the hearts and wallets of Vancouver hockey fans: the Blazers moved to Calgary. The Canucks weren't so successful in Beantown, where they lost another 14 battles in Boston Garden before finally winning one. To this day, they've yet to solve the Boston puzzle: the Bruins' home record against the Canucks is a commanding 37–7–7–1.

'72-73 NHL ALL-STARS, EAST

CENTER
☆ **PHIL ESPOSITO** BRUINS ☆

"Road trips in the '70s started with a CP Air flight to Toronto, Montreal or Los Angeles or United Airlines to Seattle. Then we sat in the terminal waiting to catch a connecting flight because there were no direct flights to the other eastern cities back then." —*JR*

"Boston Garden was very much a union building. Pittsburgh was the same. The local union rep operating the broadcast in Boston would sit and read a book or the paper during the game. To him, the game was just a perk to make some extra money; he couldn't have cared less about the game. As with most road cities, visiting radio was stuck with the assigned operator, either because he had the building contract or because of tradition." —*JR*

"Jim Hughson called the Canucks' second-ever win in Boston on radio in 1980. I missed that one because I was calling the Hockey Night in Canada game from Toronto. Because the Boston game was an afternoon affair, I tried to do both, but there were no flights." —*JR*

BOSTON

ht wing

No. 052

Date and Time: MONDAY, APRIL 7th, 1975
Place: CENTURY PLAZA HOTEL

2nd ANNUAL TEAM WIND-UP DINNER
Vancouver Blazers Hockey Team

Presentation and Announcement: 1974/75 Most V
Dancing and Entertainment to follow
Sponsored by the Century Plaz

'VER

PERIOD 1 2 3 OT

VAN 4
BOS 6 F

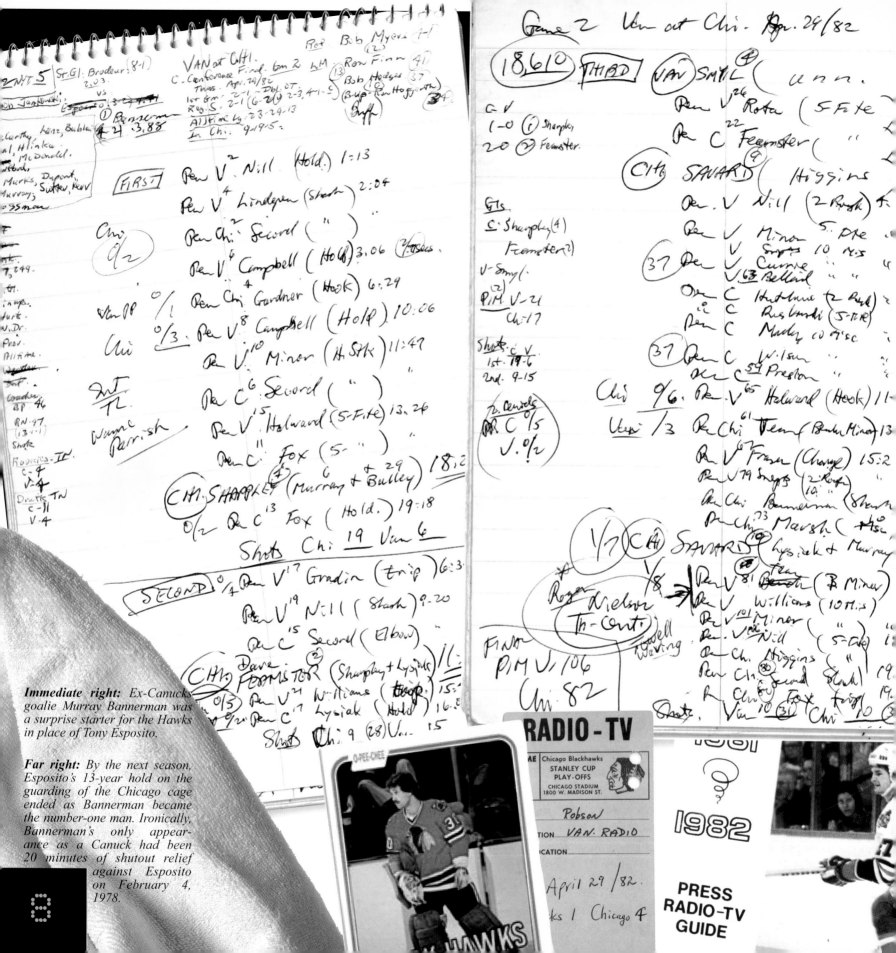

Immediate right: *Ex-Canucks goalie Murray Bannerman was a surprise starter for the Hawks in place of Tony Esposito.*

Far right: *By the next season, Esposito's 13-year hold on the guarding of the Chicago cage ended as Bannerman became the number-one man. Ironically, Bannerman's only appearance as a Canuck had been 20 minutes of shutout relief against Esposito on February 4, 1978.*

As game two of the 1982 Campbell Conference final drew to a close, Canucks coach Roger Neilson knew his team wasn't going to win. He was also frustrated by referee Bob Myers' penalty calls (and non-calls), so at 16:23 of the third period he did the logical thing: he surrendered. First one, then two, and ultimately six limp white towels hung from the hockey sticks of players on the ragtag Canucks bench. The towels hung for all to see — especially Myers. As Canucks assistant coach Ron Smith later explained, "We sent [defenceman Lars] Lindgren to centre before the face-off to tell Myers to look at our bench. We wanted to be sure he saw what we were doing."

Neilson refused to comment on the commotion he caused. But the unprecedented act was comment enough — part mocking and part show of team solidarity. When the other Canucks did eventually speak, each used different words to articulate the same feeling: respect. Respect for Neilson and respect for team. "We follow our coach," said Tiger Williams. Smith said that everyone would have joined in, "but we had run out of towels." "Roger didn't lose his head," defenceman Colin Campbell added. "When he does something like that, you know there's a useful purpose to it."

For the Canucks, the 4–1 loss at Chicago Stadium was only their second in 10 playoff games to that point — and only their second loss in 15 games (12–2–1) since Neilson had taken over as coach late in the regular season. The teams had the next day off for travel — during which the NHL fined Neilson and the Canucks $10,000. Although the league stopped short of suspending any players, in Robson's view the NHL "overreacted." But their response was nothing compared to the fan reaction that greeted the Canucks as they took to home ice for game three. Jim lights up when he thinks back to that scene: "Seeing the sight of 15,000 waving towels was something. Now, of course, you see it everywhere."

Always one to give credit where it's due, Jim adds that "John Plul, the promotions manager of CKNW, is the guy I think should be credited with the frenzied towel-waving at game three. At his urging, CKNW gave out promotional towels to fans arriving at the game."

$2.50

TONY ESPOSITO
GOALIE / GARDIEN

"The worst clock in the league was in the old Chicago Stadium. It was a circular analogue clock, and the penalty clocks were very confusing." — *JR*

"Chicago's organ was really colourful, and sat up on supports at the end of the rink. The organist, Al Melgard, would play with his back to the rink — and a man stood there watching to make sure he didn't get hit by a puck. I remember that organ made the building shake when they turned it on." The instrument was a Barton pipe organ run by a 100-hp motor with twin Spencer turbine blowers. It was capable of producing volume levels of a 2,500-instrument brass band. — *JR*

"It was rare to get to know the rink workers in the road cities, but I used to go into Chicago quite a bit when they were in Vancouver's division. There was a nice old guy, Mr. McLaughlin, who always sat outside the Hawks' dressing room in a three-piece suit. The team basically gave him the job. Every trip I'd say hello and ask, 'Is [Hawks' coach] Mr. Reay in yet?'. He always replied pleasantly, 'No, not yet, but I'll let him know you're waiting for him.'" — *JR*

CHICAGO

PERIOD 1 2 3 OT

VAN	1	
CHI	4	F

(Best-of-7 Conference Final, tied 1–1)

Ivan Hlinka

Right: Detroit's Media Guide featuring captain Reed Larson. Larson still holds the Red Wings record for most goals in a season by a defenceman (27). He was also tough and Jim's notes record that he fought Canucks rugged forward Curt Fraser in the final minute of the game.

Penalty-shot Magic in Motown
Vancouver Canucks @ Detroit Red Wings—February 11, 1982

Who says you can't coach goal-scoring? In this game, goals were exchanged early on by a pair of eventual Jack Adams Award winners (as coach of the year): Marc Crawford (1994–95 with the Quebec Nordiques) and Ted Nolan (1996–97 with the Sabres). These events were overshadowed, however, by the drama that unfolded in the third period.

With the Red Wings comfortably ahead 4–1, Canucks smooth-skating centreman Thomas Gradin was awarded a penalty shot. Robson recalls the scene vividly: "It was in the early years of Joe Louis Arena. A young Kerry Fraser was the referee. Gradin took the puck at centre, made his way to the net to my right, and made no mistake in beating Wings netminder Gilles Gilbert one on one." Make it 4–2. Close to ten minutes later, Gradin got the Canucks to within one by netting his 27th of the season.

The stage was set for a frantic finish. With Canucks goalie Richard Brodeur pulled for an extra attacker, Stan Smyl was in the clear, breaking in on the right wing, when he was hauled down by Willie Huber. Smyl was down on the ice, having hurt his right leg sliding into the post. As Fraser indicated another penalty shot, Canucks coach Harry Neale was quick

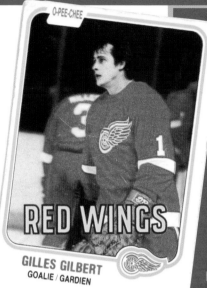

O-PEE-CHEE

RED WINGS

GILLES GILBERT
GOALIE / GARDIEN

to dispatch a messenger to tell Stan to stay down so that someone else could take the penalty shot. Jim picks up the story from there: "As Smyl was helped from the ice, Gradin came off the ice and skated around in front of the bench, like he was warming up. Fraser put the puck at centre ice. Then, unexpectedly, Ivan Hlinka jumped over the boards and promptly took the penalty shot. He put all kinds of moves on Gilbert, then shot it right from the edge of the crease while he was almost standing still. The puck went right up into the roof of the net."

The Detroit players went nuts. Danny Gare went after Fraser and was thrown out of the game. As the remaining 30 seconds ticked down, newsmen scrambled to check the record books to see if they had just witnessed history. Indeed, this is believed to be the only time in NHL history when there have been two successful penalty shots in one game, let alone one period.

"Joe Louis is a massive, old-school building. We broadcast from the very back of the seats, right along the back wall — brutal. A long ways away. The owner [Mike Ilitch, founder of Little Caesars Pizza] sells pizza so there are pizza parlours all the way around. They sell beer and pizza by the tonne. The upper-seat tickets are still cheap compared to most places, so they get a lively young crowd, drinking beer and eating pizza. It's a gold mine. Hockeytown's big." —JR

"In Detroit, the players had a regular bar that they would get the bus to stop at after the game. John Wright, Gerry O'Flaherty and I were the only ones that would stay on the bus. Today the players have a lot more money, so they probably don't drink beer; they certainly don't drink as much. Also, team camaraderie isn't like it was. Nowadays, in each road city there's a local community of people that whisk away the foreign players." —JR

"The highlight on the road was going out for a nice dinner with the guys you worked with. A lot of times you couldn't, because you're always going off to another city, often right after the game." —JR

DETROIT

PERIOD 1 2 3 OT

VAN	4	F
DET	4	

11

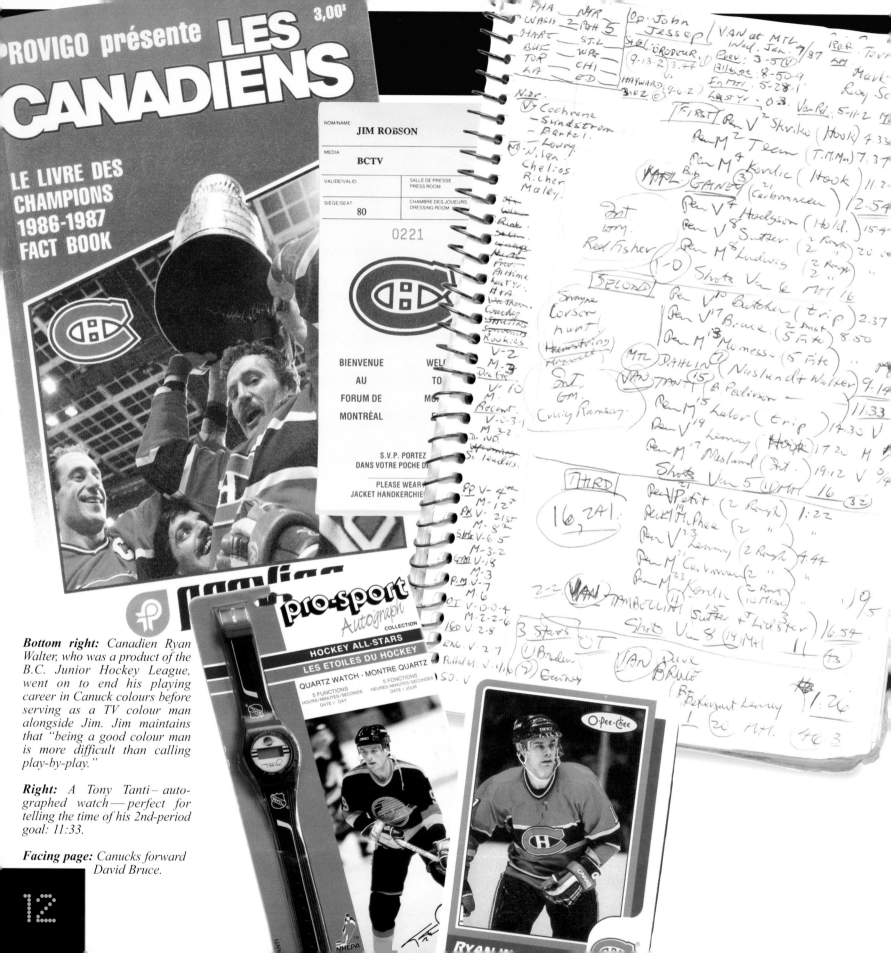

Bottom right: *Canadien Ryan Walter, who was a product of the B.C. Junior Hockey League, went on to end his playing career in Canuck colours before serving as a TV colour man alongside Jim. Jim maintains that "being a good colour man is more difficult than calling play-by-play."*

Right: *A Tony Tanti–autographed watch—perfect for telling the time of his 2nd-period goal: 11:33.*

Facing page: *Canucks forward David Bruce.*

If you're a hockey player looking for your five minutes of fame, why not do it in overtime against the defending Stanley Cup champions? Canucks utility forward David Bruce did just that against the storied Montreal Canadiens, except he didn't need the full five minutes — only 1:26. But Bruce's moment in the spotlight was made possible only because of the 44-save performance by Canucks goalie Richard Brodeur, a performance about which longtime hockey writer Tony Gallagher invoked the superlative "beyond belief."

After the game, a beaming Brodeur exclaimed, "I love to play here and I play well in Chicago. All the noisy rinks seem to be good for me. Give me some noise and I am happy." With his goal, the first game-winner and only the third of his career, Bruce seemed to be developing the same fondness for the two cities: not four weeks earlier, he had netted his first two NHL goals in the Windy City.

Jim, of course, was in Chicago that night — as he was in 1983, when he happened to be golfing with Bruce on the day the Canucks drafted him. Jim remembers being impressed with the kid: "Bruce was an outstanding minor-league player — a good, solid, character player." However, Jim acknowledges the reality that minor-league success doesn't always translate to the bigs. "His skating probably wasn't good enough to be a consistent NHL player," Jim carried on. "Instead, he was more

of a fringe, Jimmy Nill/Marc Crawford kind of player." Like Nill and Crawford, Bruce dropped his gloves from time to time, as he did in the second period when he instigated a fight with future Canuck Sergio Momesso.

Instigating that fight backfired on Bruce as Kjell Dahlin scored on the ensuing power play to put the Habs up 2–0. Montreal's first goal had been scored in the opening period by Bob Gainey, who was playing in his 1,001st career game. Guy Carbonneau picked up an assist on the Gainey goal, which came with Montreal tough guy John Kordic (ever the perfectionist with language, Jim points out that the proper Yugoslavian pronunciation is "Kor-dich") in the sin bin. Carbonneau and Gainey were arguably the best forward duo ever to jump over the boards and kill penalties.

Despite the two-goal deficit, the Canucks chipped away and got goals from Tony Tanti and Steve Tambellini to send the game into overtime. In OT, and with his parents in the stands, Brodeur thwarted another three Montreal scoring chances before Bruce grabbed the limelight — and a rare road win in the Forum.

"The Montreal Forum had the best broadcast location in the league. I sat down low very close to the ice. I could look over at the benches and the action was spectacularly lit up by bright lights." — *JR*

"I was always envious of Danny Gallivan and Dick Irvin. They called so many great Montreal players and teams. Some called them 'homers,' but it wasn't their fault that Montreal won all the time. Dick and Danny were terrific and so knowledgeable." — *JR*

"Montreal restaurants are great or character places . . . like the ham 'n' egger around the corner from Manoir Le Moyne, where we stayed. Canadiens players like Robinson and Lafleur ate in there after practice. After games, Babe Pratt took us up to Ben's for corned beef fried rice. Same location, same menu as when he played. Canucks goalie Charlie Hodge, a four-time Cup winner with Montreal, also used to take us to Moishe's in the east end for steaks." — *JR*

"After the morning skate or during a day off, I'd visit the Dominion Gallery on Sherbrooke. Old Dr. Stern would take me upstairs in an elevator and show me E.J. Hughes sketches." — *JR*

MONTREAL

PERIOD 1 2 3 OT

VAN	3	F OT
MON	2	

13

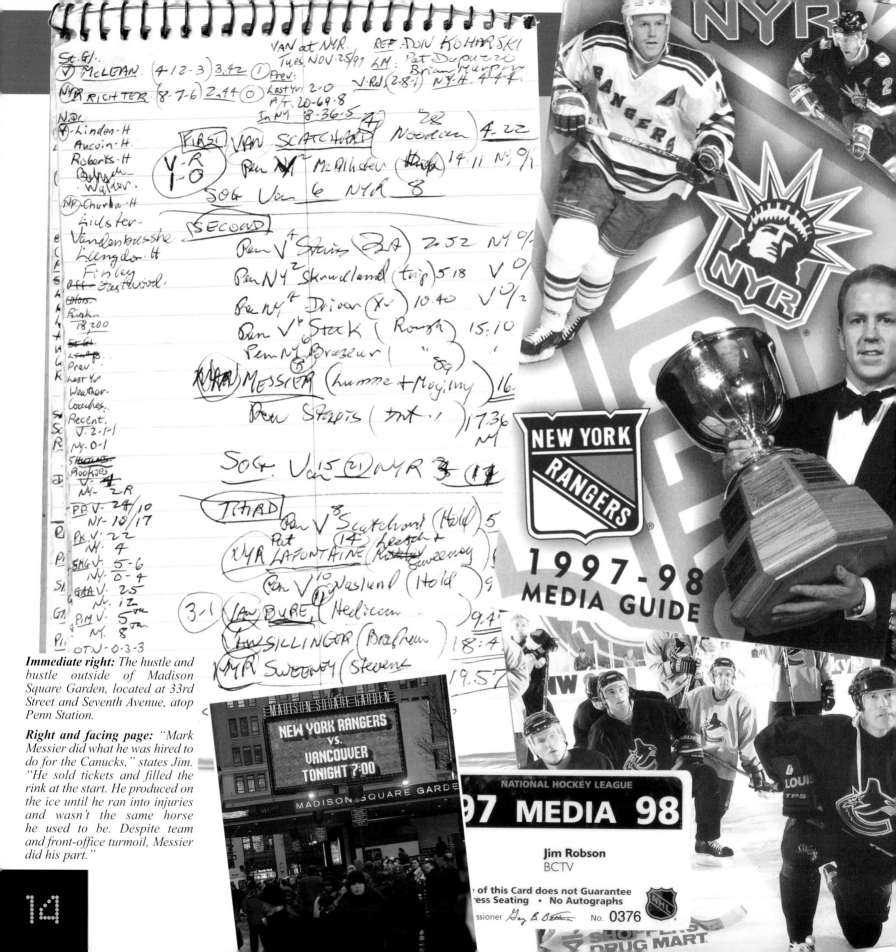

Immediate right: The hustle and bustle outside of Madison Square Garden, located at 33rd Street and Seventh Avenue, atop Penn Station.

Right and facing page: "Mark Messier did what he was hired to do for the Canucks," states Jim. "He sold tickets and filled the rink at the start. He produced on the ice until he ran into injuries and wasn't the same horse he used to be. Despite team and front-office turmoil, Messier did his part."

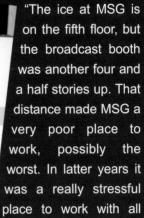

Not since Eddie Giacomin's return as a Red Wing in 1975 (only two days after the Rangers waived him) had Rangers fans welcomed home a former hero as they did on this night. The returning player was their former captain, Mark Messier, heralded as the one most responsible for bringing the Cup back to Broadway in 1994 after a 54-year drought. As his former linemate and protégé Adam Graves put it, "Any time you have a living legend like Mark Messier coming to play, it's always exciting." By game time, the emotion inside Madison Square Garden was intense, helped along by a two-minute pregame tribute to Messier that was played on the video scoreboards as the crowd chanted "Mes-sier, Mes-sier!"

Jim puts it simply: "New York is his town. He's huge there."

To start the game, Canucks bench boss and former Ranger coach Mike Keenan lined up Brian Noonan, another ex-Ranger making his first return to MSG, on Messier's right side. All three men had been prominent in the Rangers' 1994 Stanley Cup triumph over the Canucks. Interestingly, three leading Canucks from that classic seven-game final weren't in the lineup: Trevor Linden (hurt), Dave Babych and Doug Lidster (by now with the Rangers, but also injured). One Canuck from '94 who did suit up for Messier's return was Jyrki Lumme, who offered some insight into the Vancouver

team's collective feeling heading into the game: "Deep down we thought we can't blow this for Mess; he's too great a guy. We didn't have to talk about it; everybody felt the same way. We had to play well for him."

Those intentions materialized in the game. With the Canucks up 1–0, Lumme did his part by springing Messier in alone on Rangers goalie Mike Richter. From the blue line in, Messier did the rest, scoring on his old teammate and pal. After the game, Messier described his reaction to the goal: "My first thought was that we were up 2–0. My second thought was, 'Hey, I got one here!'" Messier's goal would have been the game winner had it not been for sloppy defensive play that allowed the Rangers to score with only three ticks left on the clock to make the final score 4–2 for Vancouver.

"When I left here, I left everything here," Messier said of the Big Apple. "Now it's time to move on. To try and do in Vancouver what we were able to do here. I had six great years here, and I have nothing but great memories." He added to those great memories during his homecoming game, but during Messier's three-year stay in Vancouver he was not able to repeat the magic he'd worked in Manhattan— where many fans were glad he returned as a free agent in 2000.

NEW YORK

ORCA BAY
SPORTS & ENTERTAINMENT

PERIOD 1 2 3 OT

| VAN | 4 | |
| NYR | 2 | F |

15

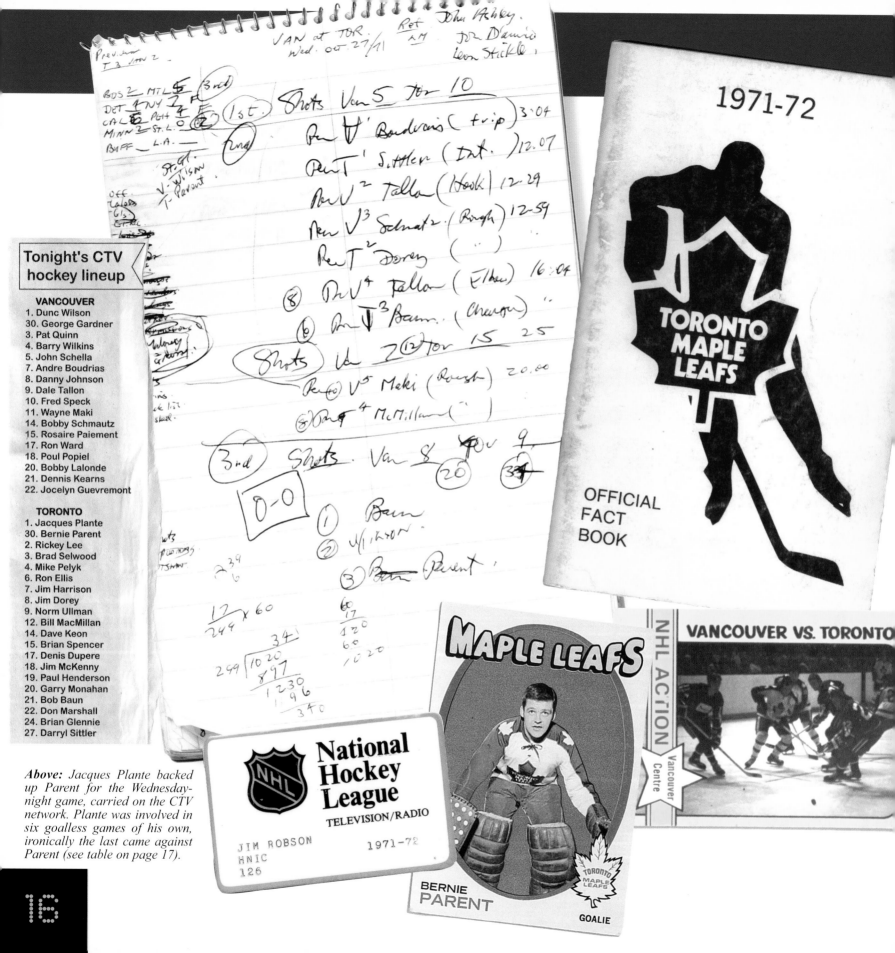

Above: Jacques Plante backed up Parent for the Wednesday-night game, carried on the CTV network. Plante was involved in six goalless games of his own, ironically the last came against Parent (see table on page 17).

1971-72

TORONTO MAPLE LEAFS

OFFICIAL FACT BOOK

National Hockey League
TELEVISION/RADIO

JIM ROBSON
HNIC
126   1971-72

MAPLE LEAFS

BERNIE PARENT
GOALIE

NHL ACTION

VANCOUVER VS. TORONTO

"**F**orwards' checking Canucks' only woe" read the game-day headline in the *Toronto Star* sports section. The article began: "Canucks' coach Hal Laycoe likes the way his defence has been performing. He lists his goal-keeping as erratic, but adequate. However, he faults his forwards for a lack of back-checking…." Yet on this night, defence, goaltending and back-checking would all be in fine form — for both teams. After the game, Laycoe called it "the purest performance we've ever had."

Despite only two minutes and 44 seconds of power-play action, the 0–0 game had plenty of scoring chances — the shots-on-goal tally was 34–20 in favour of the Leafs. "Scoreless ties usually get a negative writeup because they're considered dull," says Robson. "I guess if there are goals, then the game is easier to remember." Yet score-less ties should be memorable simply because of their rarity. From 1967–68 through to the end of the 2002–03 season, there had been only 67 goalless games played in the NHL — out of more than 30,000 matches!

The game matched two goalies with tremendous promise — the Leafs' Bernie Parent and the Canucks' Dunc Wilson, both of whom had played in the Philadelphia Flyers organization. Robson remembers always liking Dunc: "I used to call him 'Stonewall' and he would call me 'Foster'" (a reverent tip of the goal mask to legendary play-by-play man Foster Hewitt). "Dunc was a good goaltender," Robson continued,

"very competitive, but he could be his own worst enemy." As for Parent, Jim says, "Without a doubt, By the mid-'70s Parent was the best, without a doubt. It's still hard for me to picture him as a Maple Leaf because of his Flyer Cups."

Royal Bank Leo's Leaders
CANUCKS PLAYER OF THE WEEK

The numbers back Jim up. By the time Parent's career was cut short by an eye injury, he had posted 54 regular-season shutouts and another six in the playoffs. His counterpart ended up with only eight career shutouts, and none in the playoffs. (Wilson holds the dubious distinction of being the NHL goalie who played the most games without ever appearing in the playoffs.) In this game, the 88th in Canucks history, Wilson was responsible for the team's first-ever shutout. It was also Wilson's first NHL shutout, and it only took him 41 games!

WILSON AND PARENT CAREER SCORELESS GAMES IN THE NHL

March 14, 1968 Los Angeles (Terry Sawchuk) @ Philadelphia (Parent)

October 26, 1969 St. Louis (Jacques Plante) @ Philadelphia (Parent)

October 17, 1970 Philadelphia (Parent) @ Pittsburgh (Les Binkley)

October 27, 1971 Vancouver (Wilson) @ Toronto (Parent)

February 3, 1977 Pittsburgh (Wilson) @ Cleveland (Gary Simmons)

"During the 1972–73 season I got to work in the famous gondola at Maple Leaf Gardens, a few yards away from where Foster Hewitt worked. I laid out my notes and reference material as I always did, but I acciden-tally knocked the rule book and it fell sixty feet into the seats. I turned to the engineer from CFRB Toronto and said, 'I'm going to miss that thing tonight, I just know it.' Sure enough, Canucks goalie Bruce Bullock threw his stick at Ron Ellis during the game. Uproar ensued when referee Dave Newell didn't call a penalty…not that I could check the rule book for the listeners." — *JR*

"I usually called games from a little radio booth until Leafs owner Harold Ballard had it torn down without telling anyone. Thereafter I was crammed into the press box…at least the Toronto writers could hear what kind of a job I did." — *JR*

"I liked staying at the Westbury Hotel, just a few doors away from MLG. The players liked it, too, but by the '80s they got too big for the beds, so we had to move." — *JR*

TORONTO

● ● ● ●
PERIOD 1 2 3 OT

VAN	0	
TOR	0	F

17

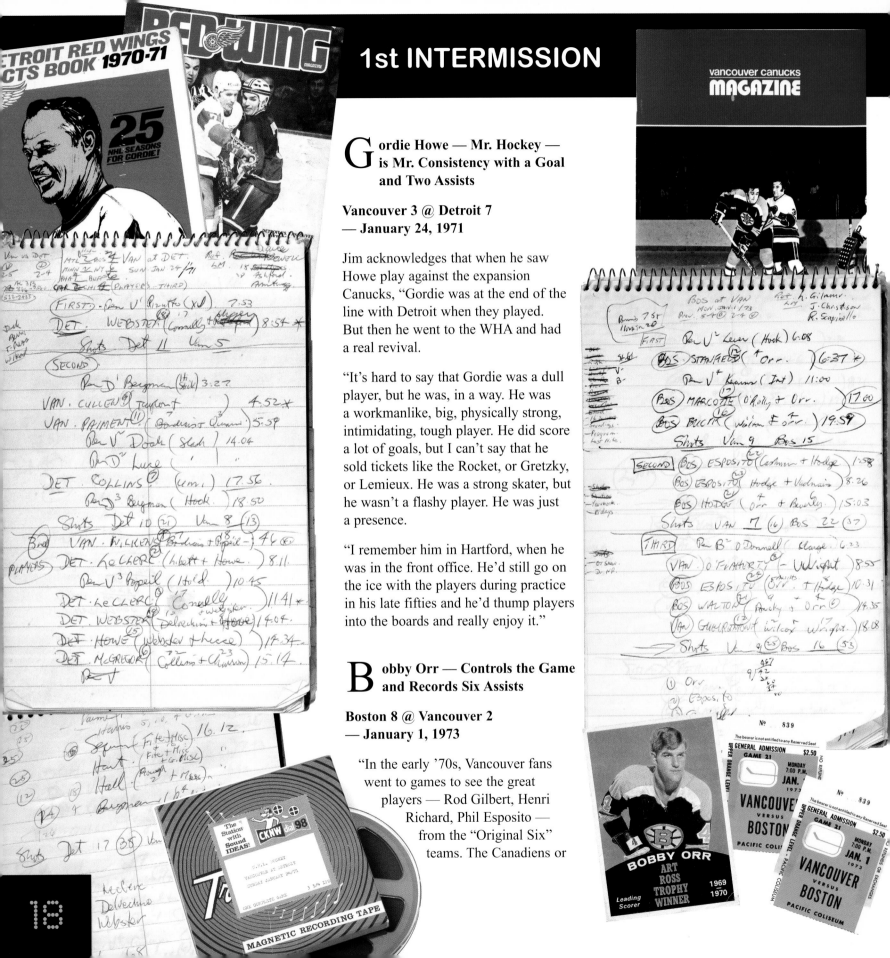

Gordie Howe — Mr. Hockey — is Mr. Consistency with a Goal and Two Assists

Vancouver 3 @ Detroit 7 — January 24, 1971

Jim acknowledges that when he saw Howe play against the expansion Canucks, "Gordie was at the end of the line with Detroit when they played. But then he went to the WHA and had a real revival.

"It's hard to say that Gordie was a dull player, but he was, in a way. He was a workmanlike, big, physically strong, intimidating, tough player. He did score a lot of goals, but I can't say that he sold tickets like the Rocket, or Gretzky, or Lemieux. He was a strong skater, but he wasn't a flashy player. He was just a presence.

"I remember him in Hartford, when he was in the front office. He'd still go on the ice with the players during practice in his late fifties and he'd thump players into the boards and really enjoy it."

Bobby Orr — Controls the Game and Records Six Assists

Boston 8 @ Vancouver 2 — January 1, 1973

"In the early '70s, Vancouver fans went to games to see the great players — Rod Gilbert, Henri Richard, Phil Esposito — from the "Original Six" teams. The Canadiens or

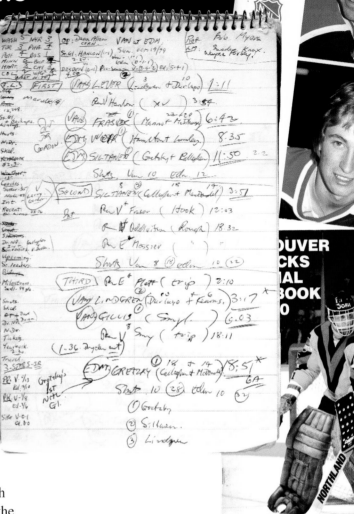

Leafs would come to town, and the Vancouver fans would cheer for them. Only if the Canucks got off to a good start would they jump over to the Canucks' bandwagon. "Over the years, Canucks fans always seemed to boo the great players — Gretzky, Frank Mahovlich and especially Bobby Orr. I remember them booing Orr on the night when he had six assists. I think the booing would get Orr so mad that he'd just take the whole game and stuff it down everybody's throats. Vancouver fans' booing was a sign of respect, but it used to bother me. They'd never do that in Montreal.

"Ted Reynolds hosted a panel show in December 1972 about the hockey highlights of the year. I said a lot of the fans out west were sorry to see the Bruins win the 1972 Stanley Cup over the Rangers because Vancouver had had a tie-in with the Rangers back in the minor-league days. The Bruins were in town when the show aired on New Year's Eve. The next night, the Bruins played the Canucks. I was doing my pregame interview with Bruins coach Tom Johnston when one of the Boston players or trainers snuck around and took my briefcase with all my notes and equipment. After the interview, one of the ushers pointed me into the dressing room, where the Bruins were waiting for me. When I went in, they really gave it to me, especially Bobby Orr. They said, 'Here comes the guy who didn't think the Bruins should have won the Cup.' I said, 'I'm just here to get my

briefcase. I was told it is in here.' And they all said, 'Oh, it can't be here.' Then the road stickboy, Dan Jukich (later the voice of Hastings Park Racetrack), caught my eye and pointed at the garbage can. So I reached in and pulled out my briefcase while all the guys threw rolled-up balls of tape at me. I felt very uncomfortable in there."

Wayne Gretzky — Scores First NHL Goal

Vancouver 4 @ Edmonton 4 — October 14, 1979

Gretzky's first NHL goal was scored on the power play with six attackers (Oilers goalie Dave Dryden was on the bench) to tie the game at 4–4 with 1:09 left. The goal came against the Canucks' young star goalie, Glen Hanlon.

"Tell you the truth, I fanned on the backhander," confessed Gretzky when discussing the goal after the game. "The puck just dribbled through [Hanlon's] pads," he continued, "but by the time the story gets back to Brantford (his hometown), I'm sure it'll be an end-to-end rush." At the time, Hanlon prophetically observed, "Only a real goal scorer would score on something like that." Jim recalls Hanlon later joking, "I created a monster!"

Hanlon became Gretzky's first victim after Tony Esposito of Chicago and Rogie Vachon of Detroit held the soon-to-be Great One goalless in his first two NHL games (although he recorded his first NHL assist in the Detroit game).

Amazingly by today's standards, there was no television broadcast of this historic game. It was carried on radio only. Gretzky was the game's first star.

Above: *Jim on the air with former Canucks player and colour man, Garry Monahan. Monahan was the first-ever #1 draft pick (by Montreal) when the NHL instituted its amateur draft in 1963.*

Right: *The way the NHL and its partners marketed hockey in Jim's early days was a far cry from the glitz and hype employed today.*

I'M A HOCKEY NUT CKNW/98

2nd p

COMMENT TO ONE M

"STAND BY FOR THE SECO
C: COMMERCIAL - CLIENT
C: COMMERCIAL - CLIENT
C: COMMERCIAL - CLIENT

Play-by-play...three 3
commercials inserted

"THE SCORE...THIS IS NH
COMMERCIAL - CLIENT

"THE SCORE...MORE HOCKE
COMMERCIAL - CLIENT

"THE SCORE....FROM (st

COMMERCIAL - CLIENT

"THE SCORE....MORE CANU
EC: COMMERCIAL - CLIENT
EC: COMMERCIAL - CLIENT

"THAT'S THE SECOND PERI
GAME. THE SCORE....A

COMMERCIAL - CLIENT
COMMERCIAL - CLIENT

mary and comment to:

VANCOUVER CANUCKS NHL HOCKEY IN THREE MINUTES"
COMMERCIAL - CLIENT   CART #
WS HEADLINES

31: COMMERCIAL - CLIENT   CART #
32: COMMERCIAL - CLIENT   CART #

Schedule of Memorable Nights

OCTOBER

		1	2	3	4	5
PIT/FLA '76 '00	7	8	DET 9	BOS 1 73	TOR 11 1970	12
13	EDM 14 1979	15	16	17	18	19
20	21	22	23	24	25	26
TOR 27 1971	28	29	30	PHO 31 2003		

NOVEMBER

					1	2
3	4	5	6	7	EDM 8 1985	9
10	QUE/MIN 11 '01	12	13	NJ 14 1996	15	16
MIN 17 1988	18	19	20	21	DAL/ATL 22 '95 / '99	23
STL 24 1990	NYR 25 1997	26	CAR 27 2002	28	29	30

HOME year AWAY year

JIM ROBSON
" what a difference a voice makes"

Campbell Expansion (1967 & Early '70s)

CEMBER

	2	3	4	5	6	7
NA	9	TOR 10 1980	11	12	13	14
	16	17	18	19	20	21
	23	24	25	26	27	SJ 28 1991
IL	30	31				

NUARY

		BOS 1 1973	2	3	COL 4 1980
6	MTL 7 1987	8	9	10	11
13	14	15	PROV 16 1968	17	18
WPG 20 1984	21	22	23	DET 24 1971	25
27	28	29	30	31	

Western Hockey League

BRUARY

						1
3	4		6	7	All Star 8 1983	
10	DET 1 1982	BUF/TB 12 '93/'94		WASH 14 1978	15	
CLEV 17 1978		19	20	BOS 21 2000	22	
24	25	26	27	28		

MARCH

	OAK 3 <TML> 1970					1
2	HART 3 1985	4	5	KC/CBJ 6 '76 '03	7	8
9	10	11	12	NYR 13 1976	14	15
16	17	18	19	20	ATL 21 1975	22
LA 23 1994	24	25	26	27	28	29
30	31					

APRIL

		1	2	3	OTT 4 1993	5
6	7	8	PHIL 10 1979	11	12	
13	CAL 14 1999	MON 15 1975	16	17	18	19
20	CAL 21 <EDM> 1988	22	23	24	25	26
27	28	CHI 29 1982	30			

<EDM> Edmonton at Calgary, "Battle of Alberta" classic

MAY

				1	2	3
4	5	6	7	NYI 8 1982	9	10
11	12	13	14	15	16	17
18	19	20	21	22	NYI 24 <PHIL> 1980	
25	26	BUF/CHI 27 <PHIL> '75 / '95	28	29	30	31

<PHIL> Philadelphia at Buffalo Sabres, 1975

JUNE

1	2	3	4	5	6	7
8	9	10	NYR 11 1994	12	13	14
15	16	17	18	19	20	21
22	23	24	25	26	27	28
29	30					

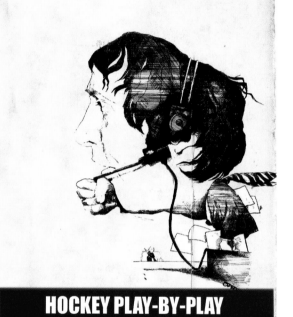

HOCKEY PLAY-BY-PLAY
Around the NHL with Jim Robson

> I never liked the term 'house broadcaster.' I described what happened, whether it was good or bad. If a guy gave the puck away for a bad goal, then he gave it away on the radio just as he did in the rink, and if the opposition made a great play, then they made a great play.

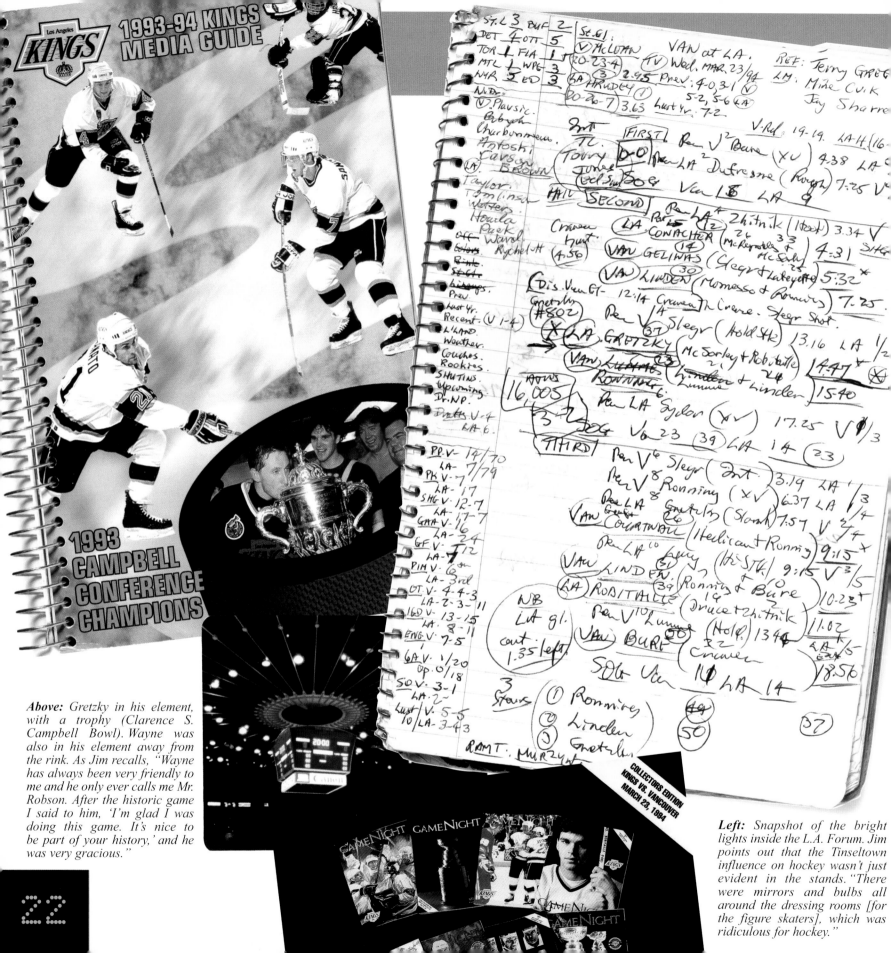

Above: *Gretzky in his element, with a trophy (Clarence S. Campbell Bowl). Wayne was also in his element away from the rink. As Jim recalls, "Wayne has always been very friendly to me and he only ever calls me Mr. Robson. After the historic game I said to him, 'I'm glad I was doing this game. It's nice to be part of your history,' and he was very gracious."*

Left: *Snapshot of the bright lights inside the L.A. Forum. Jim points out that the Tinseltown influence on hockey wasn't just evident in the stands. "There were mirrors and bulbs all around the dressing rooms [for the figure skaters], which was ridiculous for hockey."*

Jim's economy with words comes through in this, play-by-play call of the complete Wayne Gretzky shift that ended when he scored to pass Gordie Howe and become the greatest goal scorer in NHL history.

"*. . . And of course Gretzky's on the ice on the power play . . . 6:44 remaining in the second period . . . Canucks up 2–1 after having a goal disallowed. Tina Houston of North Van won $158 for the Canuck power-play goal by Martin Gelinas. Now Gretzky takes a face-off against John McIntyre . . . . Is this going to be the magic moment in Los Angeles? Gretzky out there with Kurri. McSorley moves up, too, on this face-off. Gretzky wins the draw . . . back to Sydor at the left point . . . tried to get it to the corner. Knocked down by Jyrki Lumme . . . plays it up to McIntyre and he clears it down the ice. Canuck penalty killers are McIntyre and Hunter up front; On defence, Lumme and Murzyn. As McSorley comes up the ice with the puck . . . passes to Sydor, who shoots it in. McLean missed it back of the net. Murzyn rolls it back of the goal to Jyrki Lumme . . . fails to clear it out. Sydor kept it in. Now McSorley at the right point . . . working off the point with the puck. Over to Sydor . . . watched by McIntyre. Sydor dumps it around behind the net . . . Kurri checked there. But Gretzky gets the puck in the right corner. Gretzky working off the boards . . . out to McSorley . . . Gretzky . . . Gretzky right circle . . . back to McSorley. Took a shot that is blocked. Chance for Sydor, stopped by McLean. Puck taken in the corner by McIntyre, who brings it to the neutral zone. Good effort by McIntyre to put the puck down the ice. Lost his glove, then heads to the bench on a change. One minute remaining in the penalty to Slegr. Puck brought through the middle by Sydor . . . shoots it in the Vancouver zone. Gretzky after it on the boards. Murzyn picked it off near the corner. It's loose on the end boards. Gretzky picked it up. Gretzky throws it back to the point. It is Zhitnik with a shot that is blocked. And the puck is taken by Trevor Linden. Up to Courtnall. One-on-one at centre, moving in on McSorley. Linden joins the rush . . . gets the pass, can't get a shot away. And the Kings quickly back . . . Robitaille coming in with Gretzky trailing. Gretzky gets the puck. On the right to McSorley . . . centred it to Gretzky . . . scores! Wayne Gretzky! . . . There it is, number eight-oh-two! . . . [This is followed by 37 seconds of bedlam.] All the Kings came off the bench, but there won't be a penalty tonight. . . .*"

Hearing the call played back, Jim says, "I should have put in, 'Gretzky's the greatest scorer of all time!' . . . but I never prepared my lines because I never knew what was going to happen."

LOS ANGELES KINGS

KINGS

MEDIA

Issued to: Jim Robson.

Representing: CKNW/BCTV

Date: 3-23-94

GOOD THIS DATE ONLY

VAN. 6. LA. 3.
(Gretzky scores record-setting goal #802)
RMRn

Los Angeles Kings

Non-transferable
Subject to conditions on back

"In 1984 I was doing a game in L.A. and a young guy wearing sunglasses with his collar up and his hat pulled down comes over, shakes my hand and says, 'Hi Jim, my name is Michael.' I said, 'Hi. Are you a hockey fan?' He nodded and said he was from Vancouver. So I politely asked, 'Are you going to school down here?' He replied, 'No, I'm working down here.' Anxious to watch the pregame warmup, I said, 'Well, thanks for coming by. Enjoy the game.' Former Vancouver Canadians baseball broadcaster, Rory Marcus, almost fell off the chair next to me. 'Don't you know who that is?' he said. Turns out 'Michael' was Michael J. Fox. He was at the game to watch his friends, Cam Neely and Frank Caprice of the Canucks. On the bus after the game the team gave me a hard time for not knowing who Fox was. Eventually, assistant coach Jack McIlhargey stood up and said, 'Listen, you guys: Robson didn't know Michael J. Fox, but Michael J. Fox knew Robson!'" — *JR*

LOS ANGELES

PERIOD 1 2 3 OT

VAN 6
LA 3 F

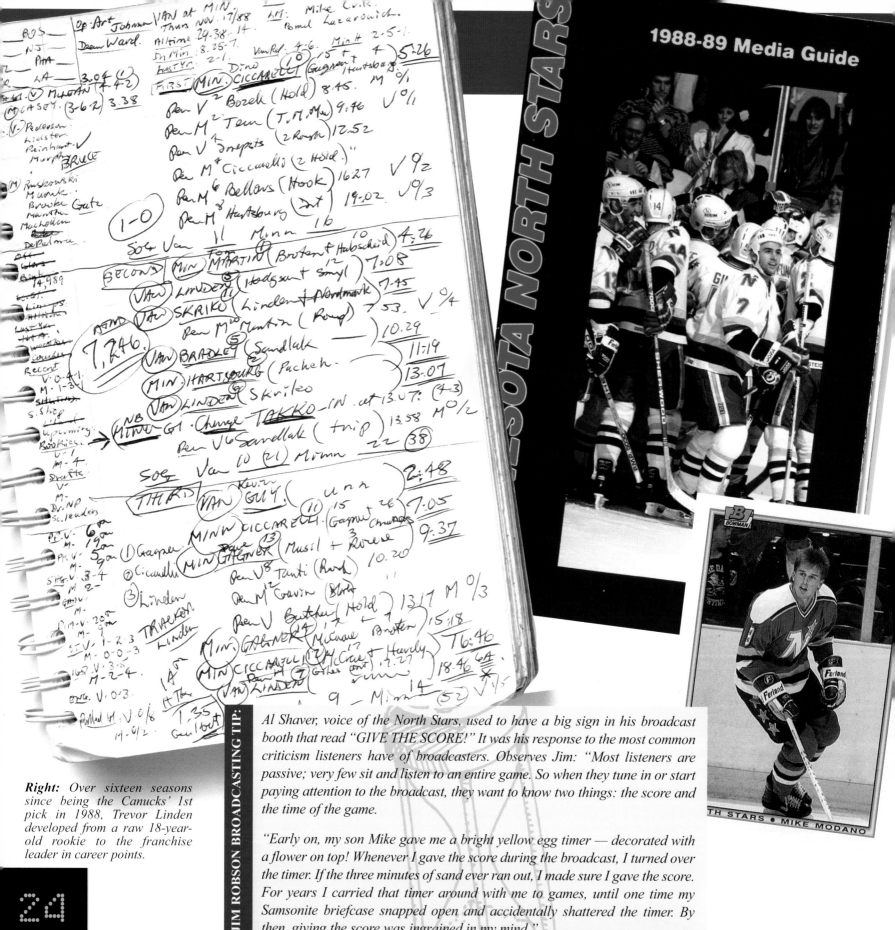

1988-89 Media Guide

MINNESOTA NORTH STARS

Right: *Over sixteen seasons since being the Canucks' 1st pick in 1988, Trevor Linden developed from a raw 18-year-old rookie to the franchise leader in career points.*

JIM ROBSON BROADCASTING TIP:

Al Shaver, voice of the North Stars, used to have a big sign in his broadcast booth that read "GIVE THE SCORE!" It was his response to the most common criticism listeners have of broadcasters. Observes Jim: "Most listeners are passive; very few sit and listen to an entire game. So when they tune in or start paying attention to the broadcast, they want to know two things: the score and the time of the game.

"Early on, my son Mike gave me a bright yellow egg timer — decorated with a flower on top! Whenever I gave the score during the broadcast, I turned over the timer. If the three minutes of sand ever ran out, I made sure I gave the score. For years I carried that timer around with me to games, until one time my Samsonite briefcase snapped open and accidentally shattered the timer. By then, giving the score was ingrained in my mind."

TH STARS • MIKE MODANO

The game was to feature the top two picks in the previous June's amateur draft: #1 Mike Modano of the North Stars versus the #2 selection, Trevor Linden of the Canucks. The only problem was that someone forgot to give Modano and the North Stars the script. The centreman had returned to junior hockey after he and Minnesota had been unable to come to terms on a contract, so the stage on this night belonged exclusively to the 18-year-old rookie, Linden.

Playing in only his 21st career game, Linden set about making his mark. In a high-scoring seesaw affair, Linden got his club on the scoreboard at 7:08 of the second and again at 13:07, sending North Stars goalie Jon Casey to the showers and the Canucks to their dressing room up 4–3 after 40 minutes. Early in the third, Canuck defenceman Kevin Guy scored his first NHL goal, giving the Canucks a two-goal cushion. Jim gives a glimpse of his decency when he comments that, "When a youngster [like 23-year-old Guy] got his first goal, I'd often go tell the kid, 'I'll see if I can get you a copy of the radio call of your goal,' and then I'd have the engineer make a cassette tape of it and give it to the player later on." But on this night

16

Trevor Linden
FORWARD

MOHAWK

Guy's goal wouldn't be a factor: Minnesota rattled off four straight goals, two each by Dave Gagner and Dino Ciccarelli. Ciccarelli's last one gave him a hat trick.

Undaunted, the rookie Linden went back to work, putting the finishing touch on a hat trick of his own — the first of his young career — scoring with 1:14 left in the game to pull the Canucks within one. But time ran out on the Canucks. The final score was 7–6 for Minnesota. The buzz after the game wasn't about the result, but about Linden. Jim remembers the media reaction the next morning: "The Minnesota papers second-guessed North Stars management, asking, 'Did they get the wrong guy? Because our kid is back in junior and won't sign and Vancouver's pick looks great.'"

Linden did look great, and he followed up his Minnesota hat trick with a second one, this time at home, just three games later in a 4–2 win against Buffalo. He ended his rookie campaign with 30 goals, and Robson concludes, "Although in the long run Modano turned out to be a great player, Linden has been every bit as valuable a draft choice."

"Minnesota is good hockey country with a tremendous following for local high school and college hockey. The Met Center was a funny rink with unusual seats. Each seat was They were coloured black, white, green or yellow and the colours were scattered around the rink in random order." — *JR*

"The Canucks used to stay in a hotel right next to the Met Center. During one visit, there was a huge blizzard. So, as is often the case, the road team was ready to play but the home team and the fans couldn't get to the rink. Nonetheless, the Canucks coaches had the players brave the elements and walk to the rink with their gear. I held my briefcase in front of my face just to get through the wind and snow. At 8:00 p.m., instead of a league game, the Canucks had an East-West intrasquad game. The guys had a fun time; it was a nice break in the gruelling road schedule." — *JR*

"In the early 1980s, Minnesota had some great marketing ideas. They were the first to project ads on the ice between periods. I thought every team would do it, but it never took off." — *JR*

MINNESOTA

PERIOD 1 2 3 OT

VAN 6
MIN 7   F

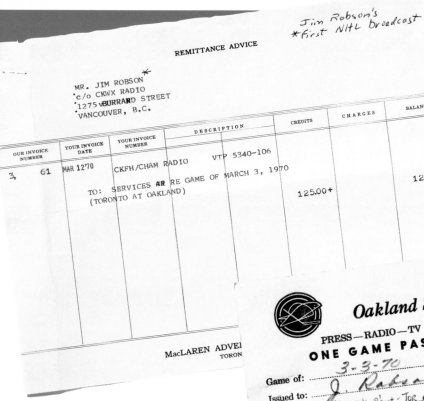

Jim Robson's
*First NHL Broadcast

MR. JIM ROBSON
c/o CKWX RADIO
1275 BURRARD STREET
VANCOUVER, B.C.

OUR INVOICE NUMBER	YOUR INVOICE DATE	YOUR INVOICE NUMBER	DESCRIPTION	CREDITS	CHARGES	BALANCE
3, 61	MAR 12'70	CKFH/CHAM RADIO VTP 5340-106				125.00 *
			TO: SERVICES RE GAME OF MARCH 3, 1970 (TORONTO AT OAKLAND)	125.00+		

MacLAREN ADVER
TORO

Bottom right: *Game-day telegram sent to Jim by his former co-workers and by Canucks PR man Greg Douglas and Joe Crozier, former coach of the WHL Canucks.*

Facing right: *Paul Henderson netted two goals including the game winner, part of his 10-goal outburst in March 1970 to end the season at 20 goals.*

NHL summaries

TORONTO 4, OAKLAND 1
First Period

No scoring
Penalties-Roberts Oak 2:10. Ley T. 7:58, Harrison T, O'Donoghue Oak. 10:44, Glennie T 13:37

Second Period
1 Toronto, Ellis 28 (Henderson, Pelyk) 5:30
2 Toronto, Henderson 11 (Ullman, Ley) 12:20
3 Toronto, Keon 28 (Oliver) 16:41
Penalties-Dorey T, 2:54, McKenny T 6:23. Roberts Oak 15:20.

Third Period
4 Toronto, Henderson 12 (Ullman, Pelyk) 2:32
5 Oakland, O'Donoghue 3 (Ferguson, Roberts) 19:17
Penalties-Armstrong T., 10:57, Jarrett Oak, 14:11

Attendance at Oakland, 4,989

Oakland Seals
1969/70 Factbook
One Dollar

MIKE LAUGHTON

JR's 1st
NHL B'cast
TOR at OAK.
Mar 3, 1970

Oakland Seals
PRESS—RADIO—TV
ONE GAME PASS
Game of: 3-3-70
Issued to: J. Robson
(1st NHL B'cast - TOR at OAK)
Authorized:
William N. Creasy

Nº 447

William N. Creasy, Jr., Pr

NATIONAL HOCKEY LEAGUE
Official Magazine

western union
Telegra

857P PST MAR 3 70 LB402
L OLB402 (RAA027) CPRZCZCRBWWRPZC 17 3NEX SIG RX   CPT FD VANCOUV
BC 3 656P PST

JIM ROBSON CARE OAKLAND COLISEUM
HOCKEY ARENA OAKLAND CALIF

BEST OF LUCK. WE ARE ALL PULLING FOR YOU. SEE YOU IN THE NHL.
MARY AND GREG MARJ AND JOE.
(Douglas)   (Crozier)

CPCN TEL VCR B
CKWX VCR

MAR 3 '04   2:15 PM

JIM ROBSON
EDGEWATER HOTEL
OAKLAND CALIFORNIA

WE KNOW YOU WILL BE ENCHANTING
NOW THAT YOU ARE GALLIVAN-TING
AND WE KNOW THAT YOU CAN DO IT
BETTER STILL THAN YOUNG BILL HEWITT
ALL THE GANG HERE WISH YOU WELL
SO GET OUT THERE AND GIVE THEM HOCKEY

BEST WISHES FROM ALL THE GANG AT C

As the regular season wound down for the East Division's last-place Leafs, Jim got his big-league break. It came in the form of a call from the Leafs' broadcast agency, MacLaren Advertising. Jim knew the reason for the call. "They wanted to test-drive me. Rather than send Foster Hewitt out to Oakland, they wanted a Vancouver guy, knowing they had to go into Vancouver the next year with Hockey Night in Canada. They wanted to know if I could do the games." Jim Robson had made it to the NHL, MacLaren's questions were answered, and NHL hockey fans would reap the benefits for many years.

On this night, the young Leafs' defence was strong. So strong, in fact, that goalie Marv Edwards came within 43 seconds of earning his first NHL shutout. The Toronto blue line's performance served as a tribute to forty-year-old All-Star defenceman Tim Horton, who had been traded to the Rangers before the game. In those days the stars didn't get traded much and Horton, who had been in the Leafs organization since 1947 and played on four Cup winners, was a big star.

Upon arriving to broadcast his first NHL game, Jim was assigned the task of interviewing Horton. "Nobody knew who I was, so I waited outside the Leafs' dressing room," recalls Jim. "Finally the door opens up and Tim Horton walks by me, all dressed up in a top coat, suit and tie. Nowadays there would be a press conference, but then there was no media there, just me. I followed him under the stands with my mike and a battery-powered reel-to-reel tape machine over my shoulder.

PAUL HENDERSON
MAPLE LEAFS

"After I called out to him several times, he finally turned around. He had tears flowing down his face. I said, 'I'm Jim Robson from Vancouver, broadcasting for Leafs radio. They asked me to do an interview with you, but I don't think now is the right time.' So I chickened out. I'll always remember big Tim Horton, bawling away like a baby after having just said goodbye to his teammates. We never talked about that incident again....I would hope he remembered how I handled it."

On a night when his trade overshadowed the game, the veteran Horton got a glimpse of one of the rookie Robson's eventual trademarks — his gentlemanly professionalism.

"The Seals played at the Oakland Coliseum, which is part of the same complex where the football Raiders and baseball Athletics play. The rink is in no-man's-land; it borders on a freeway, east of downtown Oakland, in the shadows of the San Mateo Bridge. You could see the arena from our hotel, but you couldn't walk to it because of the freeway; so we had to take a cab about four blocks to the rink. Because we were on a freeway rather than in the city, it was never an enjoyable place to go or work." — *JR*

"The Oakland Coliseum was built in the late 1960s, with no broadcasting facilities. I broadcast games from a makeshift platform area in the seats at mid-level. I remember looking behind me and seeing just row upon row of empty seats. It was never a very exciting place to go because the crowds were small. The first year after expansion, Oakland was picked to be a contender, but they never had any scoring. So fan interest in the Seals was low, and the feeling even by 1970 was that they might have to move." — *JR*

OAKLAND

INGARFIELD
SEALS
CENTER

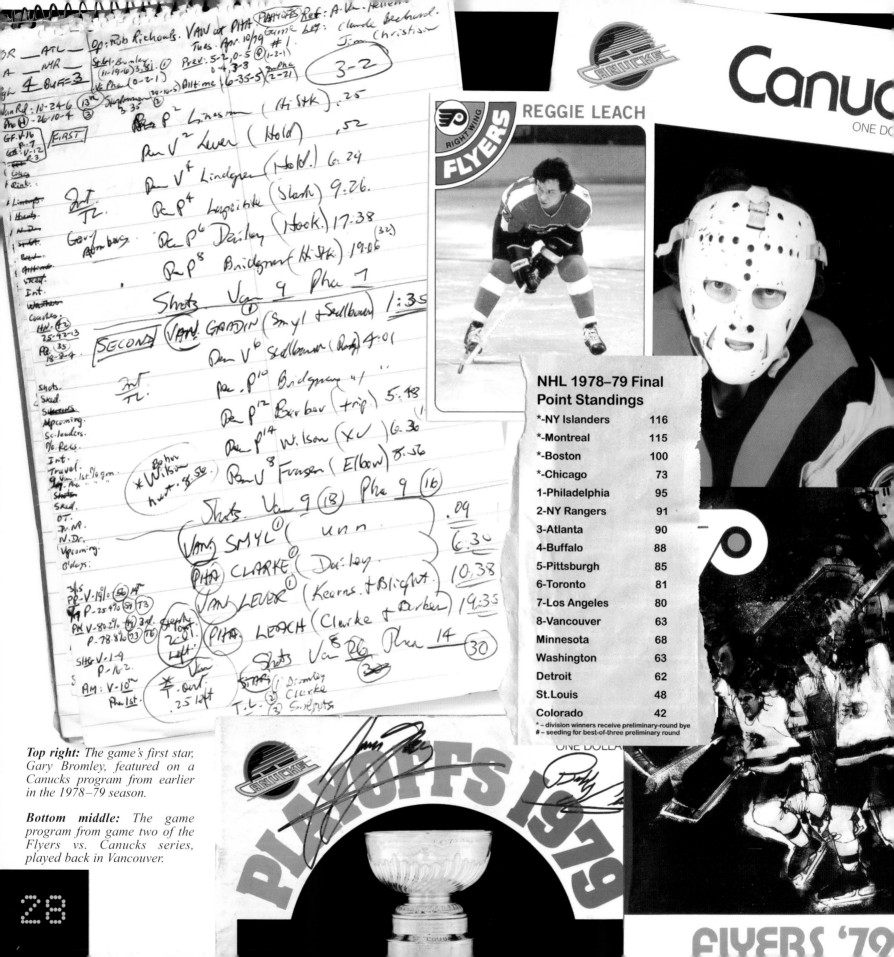

REGGIE LEACH

FLYERS RIGHT WING

Canucks ONE DO...

NHL 1978–79 Final Point Standings

*-NY Islanders	116
*-Montreal	115
*-Boston	100
*-Chicago	73
1-Philadelphia	95
2-NY Rangers	91
3-Atlanta	90
4-Buffalo	88
5-Pittsburgh	85
6-Toronto	81
7-Los Angeles	80
8-Vancouver	63
Minnesota	68
Washington	63
Detroit	62
St.Louis	48
Colorado	42

* – division winners receive preliminary-round bye
# – seeding for best-of-three preliminary round

Top right: *The game's first star, Gary Bromley, featured on a Canucks program from earlier in the 1978–79 season.*

Bottom middle: *The game program from game two of the Flyers vs. Canucks series, played back in Vancouver.*

PLAYOFFS 1979

FLYERS '79

Near Philly Upset Prompts Change to Playoff Format
Vancouver Canucks @ Philadelphia Flyers–April 10, 1979

The Canucks had no business making the playoffs in 1978–79, but a quirk in the playoff format allowed the second-place finishers in the lowly Smythe Division to leapfrog the stronger Minnesota North Stars into the post-season. The Canucks also benefited from the regular-season schedule: they played each of their division rivals eight times, including the cellar-dwelling Blues and Rockies. The Canucks piled up a record of 10–2–4, accounting for nearly 40 per cent of their paltry 63 points, against those two. By contrast, the mighty Philadelphia Flyers were among the league's elite, compiling the fourth-best record in the NHL. They had 15 more wins than the Canucks and 32 more points, so the best-of-three preliminary-round series looked like a mere tune-up for the Flyers.

The series quickly became a lesson in humility for the Flyers and a wake-up call to the league brass. Stellar goaltending by Gary "Bones" Bromley and spirited play by Canucks rookies Thomas Gradin, Curt Fraser and Stan Smyl had the visiting underdogs looking good. Gradin opened the scoring in the second period by deking Flyers goalie Wayne Stephenson to complete a pretty two-on-one with Smyl. "Steamer" got in on the scoring himself, only nine seconds into the third period, tying the NHL playoff record for fastest goal to start a period (since broken). From there the Canucks hung on and got the eventual winner

from Don Lever. The Flyers swarmed the Canucks for the final 2:01 with Stephenson pulled, but when the horn sounded they found themselves down a goal and a game.

The series shifted to Vancouver, where Flyer fortunes got even more desperate. The referee wasn't allowing the Flyers to intimidate the Canucks, as they had become accustomed to doing over the years. As Jim recounts, "Flyers executive Keith Allen went into the referee's room after the first period of game two and gave referee Dave Lewis an earful, after which Lewis put his whistle in his pocket." The Canucks managed to stay with the Flyers until the last minute of the third. With the score tied 4–4, Bobby Clarke cleanly won a draw from Gradin, and Reggie Leach scored on a one-timer. Philadelphia went on to win game three easily, but the outmatched Canucks had put a real scare into them.

Just as Flyers boss Allen had given NHL officials an earful behind closed doors in game two, it is believed he did the same at the next board of governors meetings when the topic of playoff formats was broached. The next year, the league extended the preliminary round to a best-of-five series. That system remained in place until 1986, when the first-place Flyers were upset in five games by a Ranger team that finished 32 points in arrears. Perhaps (but not likely) coincidentally, first-round series were extended to best-of-seven the year after that.

"I remember Joe Watson was devastated to be claimed by Philly in the [1967] expansion draft. After the draft, the city held a welcoming parade for the new Flyers. Joe and the Flyer players rode in open cars. Joe told me that the police patrolling the parade on horseback warned him to get down in the car if he heard gunshots! Naturally, this was worrying to a small-town guy like Joe, who was from Smithers, B.C." — *JR*

"Philly food is renowned, but to me their cheesesteak is just a glorified hot dog. The broadcast guys didn't eat in the rink. Instead, we would eat in the Press Club. In later years my wife Bea once came with me to Philadelphia. We stayed at the Sheraton in Society Hill, which is the old part of the city with cobbled streets. There we enjoyed some of the seafood restaurants." — *JR*

"Philadelphia's anthem singer is the daughter of former Flyers broadcaster Gene Hart. Hart was hands-on in the broadcast booth and he didn't like the Canucks." — *JR*

PHILADELPHIA

PERIOD 1 2 3 OT

VAN 3
PHIL 2

F

29

(Canucks lead best-of-3 series, 1–0)

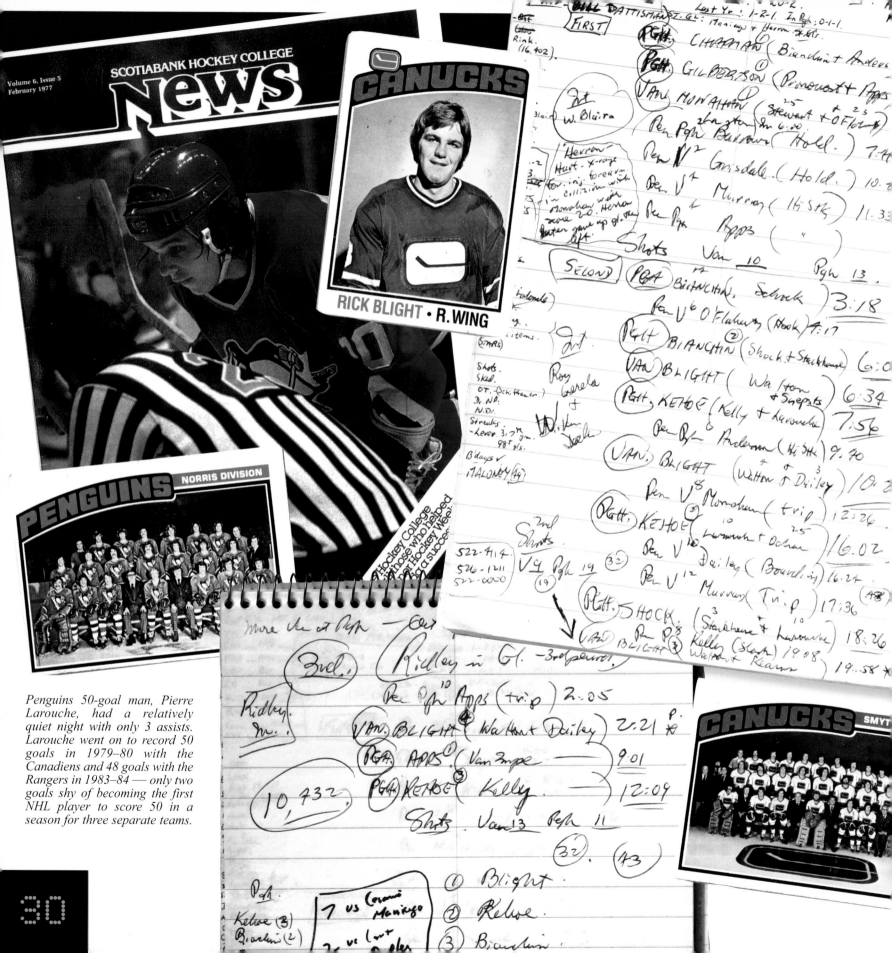

Penguins 50-goal man, Pierre Larouche, had a relatively quiet night with only 3 assists. Larouche went on to record 50 goals in 1979–80 with the Canadiens and 48 goals with the Rangers in 1983–84 — only two goals shy of becoming the first NHL player to score 50 in a season for three separate teams.

A Wild Night Inside The Igloo
Vancouver Canucks @ Pittsburgh Penguins–October 6, 1976

All teams can afford to be optimistic on opening night, and as the Canucks entered the '76–'77 schedule, they were entertaining playoff aspirations. And why not? Their revamped forward lines had some punch (Rick Blight, Mike Walton and Don Lever; John Gould, Chris Oddleifson and Dennis Ververgaert; and Andy Spruce, Garry Monahan and Gerry O'Flaherty, with Ron Stewart and Ron Sedlbauer in reserve). Add to that a promising defensive core backstopped by newly acquired netminder Cesare Maniago, and the Canucks felt ready to take on all comers — including the double blue of Pittsburgh.

But the first goal of the game should have been a tip-off that they weren't quite so ready. It's not often that a player scores a goal on his first NHL shift, and it's all but unheard of that he would be assisted by another rookie also carving up his first NHL ice. But that's how it happened for Blair Chapman and Russ Anderson at 3:02 of the first period. And so began a game Jim Robson recalls as "one of the wildest games I ever called."

The Penguins went up 2–0 only 95 seconds later, before Monahan — Jim's eventual colour man in the early 1980s — got the first Canucks goal of the season. The goal, though pretty, was somewhat tainted: earlier in the shift, Penguins' goalie Denis Herron came out to poke-check Monahan and Monahan crashed into him and broke Herron's arm. It wasn't until Monahan eventually scored on the lame Herron

that play was stopped and Herron was able to be helped from the ice. Like Maniago, Herron was starting his first game since being acquired in the off-season. Like Herron, Maniago would not finish the game, although he did stick around for two full periods, facing 32 shots and surrendering seven goals. Maniago's departure resulted in a rare occasion when all four goalies who dressed actually played.

With Herron lost, former New Westminster Bruins goalie Gord Laxton went between the pipes for Pittsburgh. Over the remaining 54 minutes of play, Laxton stopped everything — except four shots by Rick Blight! Yet in this contest, the Penguins never trailed. Up 7–4 after two periods, the Penguins kept up the pressure against Canucks backup goalie Curt Ridley, who played despite a nagging bruised finger on his catching hand. Coach Phil Maloney explained the decision to yank Maniago: "We had two defencemen chasing the puck in the corners so often I had to get Cesare out of there to save his life." The wild night came to an end with Rick Kehoe scoring to complete a hat trick of his own and to warm the hearts of the Igloo faithful.

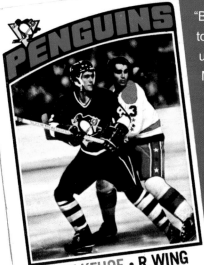

RICK KEHOE • R.WING

PITTSBURGH

PERIOD 1 2 3 OT

VAN 5
PITT 9
F

31

ST. LOUIS BLUES 1990-91 MEDIA GUIDE

Recognition: *Jim kept detailed team and player records. Here his game-by-game summary of player awards shows that Canucks defenceman Don Gibson's cross-checking minor was apparently enough to earn him GMC Tracker Player of the Game — probably the only recognition he received in his 14-game NHL career.*

Game notes: *Jim's notes indicate that Blues GM Ron Caron was Garry Monahan's 1st intermission radio guest. Jim worked in a booth that had Caron on one side and Blues broadcaster Dan Kelly on the other. Kelly had a loud, strong voice that even fans in the stands could hear, while the explosive Caron used to pound his fist on the walls if things didn't go well for the Blues.*

Media guide: *In 1990–91 Blues goalie Vincent Riendeau suffered the "curse of the media guide cover." He was traded at the start of the following season, in large part because of the emergence of Curtis Joseph.*

Brett Hull
St. Louis Blues®

SEASON		GP	G	A	TP	PIM
1987-88	CGY/STL	65	32	32	64	16
	St. Louis	78	41	43	84	33
1988-89	St. Louis	78	72	41	113	24
1989-90	St. Louis	80	86	45	131	22
1990-91	St. Louis	78	232	161	393	95
CAREER NHL TOTALS		306	232	161	393	95

BRETT HULL BECAME ONLY THE THIRD PLAYER IN NHL HISTORY TO SCORE MORE THAN 80 GOALS IN A SINGLE SEASON IN 1990-91. HULL LED THE LEAGUE IN GOALS (29), SHOTS POWER-PLAY GOALS (29), GAME-WINNING GOALS (11), SHOTS (389) AND FIRST GOALS (19). "GOLDEN BRETT" WAS AWARDED THE HART TROPHY AND ELECTED TO THE FIRST ALL-STAR TEAM IN 1990-91. HE ALSO FIRED FOUR HAT TRICKS AND TIED FOR THE BLUES' TEAM LEAD WITH A PLUS/MINUS OF +23.

BIRTHPLACE: BELLEVILLE, ONTARIO
BIRTHDATE: AUGUST 9, 1964
HEIGHT: 5' 10" WEIGHT: 201 LBS. SHOOTS: RIGHT

215
RIGHT WING

Pro Set © NHL & NHLPA 1991

Blues' Golden Brett Earns His Wings
Vancouver Canucks @ St. Louis – November 24, 1990

The Blues' Brett Hull enjoyed a remarkable season in 1990–91. He scored 86 goals — a total no one has surpassed since, and which, at the time, was bested only by the Great One (92 goals in 1981–82 and 87 in '83–'84). Hull's average of better than a goal a game was helped by numerous multiple-goal games — one of which came at home against the Canucks. On this occasion, Hull scored his 22nd and 23rd of the season to break a 1–1 tie and put the Blues up 3–1. The Canucks would eventually battle back to earn a 3–3 draw. Greg Adams scored the game-tying goal at 18:33 of the third period with Brett, uncharacteristically, in the penalty box.

The game's scoring summary bears an uncanny resemblance to one from 20 seasons before. On Valentine's Day of 1971, the expansion Canucks were in Chicago, tied 1–1, when Bobby Hull scored two goals to put the Hawks ahead 3–1, though on that occasion the score would hold up for the home side. The senior Hull's first goal on that night was a milestone — the 545th of his career, moving him past Maurice Richard into second place on the all-time goal-scoring list behind only Mr. Hockey himself, Gordie Howe. Diminutive Charlie Hodge was the Canucks goalie who surrendered the milestone goal. Coincidentally, on November 10, 1963, Hodge was tending the Canadiens' net when he was victimized on Howe's 545th career marker.

Having seen both generations of Hulls play in their prime, Jim offers an interesting comparison. "Bobby and Brett Hull are an amazing father/son act," he begins. "Both are very friendly, approachable, and say what they think. They're both great with their fans — Bobby in particular loves to sign autographs. The game couldn't have two greater ambassadors. On the ice, both were the kind of players that you would notice on every shift because they were always a threat to score a goal. Even though Brett has amassed more goals, I still think Bobby was a little more prominent in his prime."

Bobby's final tally of 610 NHL goals now ranks 12th on the all-time list. He might have rated higher, but his decision to jump to the WHA in 1972 curtailed his NHL output. Meanwhile, the younger Hull's two goals against Vancouver on this night put him at 255 for his career — in just his fourth full NHL season. As of the end of the 2003–04 campaign, Hull holds down third place on the all-time scoring list with 741 goals in 1,264 regular-season games. "Not bad for someone that no one expected to make it," declares Jim. "Brett almost quit as a kid while playing for the North Shore juveniles and working at Super Valu in North Vancouver. Lo and behold, he's one of the great goal scorers of all time. What a humble start. It's nice to see because Brett's a good guy — doesn't take himself or his success too seriously."

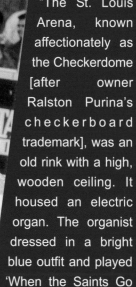

Brett Hull
NHL PRO SET PLAYER OF THE YEAR AWARD

"The St. Louis Arena, known affectionately as the Checkerdome [after owner Ralston Purina's checkerboard trademark], was an old rink with a high, wooden ceiling. It housed an electric organ. The organist dressed in a bright blue outfit and played 'When the Saints Go Marching In' while the Blues came on the ice. After the game, when the fans had gone home and the guys were working on the ice, the organist still played. He'd do a little number to say good night to the crew and they'd all yell up to him." — *JR*

"St. Louis had a real impact on the league. The Blues put in amenities like a lounge and about three different bars. Most of the other arenas didn't have that in those days. Fans would go to the bars and restaurants in the rink before the game, between periods, and after the game. The Blues were the first to issue a special card to season-ticket holders that allowed them to run up a food and booze tab." — *JR*

ST. LOUIS

Professionalism *and Broadcasting* Style

"*I was more interested in the traditional paint-the-picture style of broadcasting, with an emphasis on accuracy. Today, the emphasis has to be on show business and having a shtick. Some broadcasters today get frantic just describing the national anthem.*

"*I didn't go out of my way to criticize guys, but I certainly felt my job was to describe what happens — whether it was good or bad for the home team. Nevertheless, one night Canucks tough guy Randy Holt was extremely upset with me after Barry Beck beat him up in a fight because in Randy's mind, he never lost a fight. Holt was waiting for me after the game; in his opinion I was the Canucks' broadcaster and I shouldn't say anything negative about the team or its players. I really thought Holt was going to punch me out, and I couldn't have done anything about it if he did!*

"*I never had anyone tell me what to say or what not to say. Former Canucks owner Coley Hall tried to intimidate me one time. He phoned me, was upset because I [criticized] the team for busing the players down to Portland to avoid paying them meal money. He tried to get me off the broadcast. A colleague of mine, Mike Tytherleigh, was sitting beside me saying, 'Don't take that. Don't take that.' I was shaking like a leaf because Coley was an intimidating guy and he was the big boss, but he wasn't the boss of the radio station. I said, 'I work for the radio station, Coley. I don't work for the hockey club. And what I do for the radio station is separate from when I do a hockey game.'*

"*When John McKitrick worked at CKNW as a newsman, I'd say to him, 'Hey John, give me a critique on the broadcast tonight.' The next morning in my mailbox would be a written critique of my broadcast. He knew hockey, he knew broadcasting and he listened to every game. I knew I would always get an honest critique from John.*"

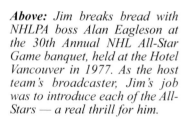

Above: *Jim breaks bread with NHLPA boss Alan Eagleson at the 30th Annual NHL All-Star Game banquet, held at the Hotel Vancouver in 1977. As the host team's broadcaster, Jim's job was to introduce each of the All-Stars — a real thrill for him.*

Game *day* Routine *– At Home*

"*On home game days I would leave home about 9:30 and go to the rink. The Canucks usually skated at 10:00. In the Coliseum I'd sit up in the corner with Babe Pratt and watch. Later in GM Place, I'd watch from down near the bench so I could jump over the rail and go right into the dressing room without having to hike a long way. Near the end of the practice, I'd go in and talk to the visiting guys. Since I saw the home guys all the time, I always thought it was more important to get some stuff from the visiting team. Somewhere in there I'd phone in a report for the noon sports from a pay phone. For many years I did a taped show with the Canucks coach, 'The Canuck Report.' I usually drove the tape to CKNW to dub it onto reel-to-reel or a cartridge so the station could run it at suppertime. From there I'd drive home for lunch around 1:30 and prepare my pregame information [see pages 2–3, The Pregame Warmup]. Often I'd then have an afternoon nap, although at home that wasn't always so easy. Then I'd get up, shower and shave, and dress up. For home games I liked to get to the rink about two hours before game time, so I left the house about 4:45 for a 7:00 o'clock game.*

"*It was important to watch the game-day skates because sometimes the coaches wouldn't tell you anything about their lineups. I watched to see which players would practise longer, knowing they weren't going to play in the game. For instance, usually the goalie that left the ice last wouldn't be the starter that night. Roger Neilson was the first coach I saw who didn't let his players wear numbers for the practices, so the media guys would have a hard time identifying everybody. On the other hand, the Montreal Canadiens used to practise in their full uniforms — mind you, their players were very familiar anyway.*"

Game day Routine – On the Road

"*The routine on the road was completely different. You're totally engrossed [in preparation], because there's nothing else to do. Before I left for a road trip, I'd get out the team cards that I last used and take them with me, because I could probably reuse or update them. The pregame routine might change on the road if there were three games in four nights, in which case there generally wasn't a game-day skate. Even then, I usually went to the rink on game day because I almost always interviewed the opposing coach. Back at the hotel, I always had a nap, and I usually phoned the home radio guy at his home and we would share information. In places like Chicago I was so isolated that I had to hike down and get the stats from the press room myself. Unlike at home, I always had a postgame show on the road, and sometimes it was a scramble to get down for the team bus. I seldom missed it, but when I did I had to take a cab back to the hotel. After road games I usually talked to the Canucks players. If they lost, it was really quiet on the bus, but after a win the players were talkative.*"

Above: *Jim prepares for an upcoming broadcast en route to the next road game.*

Broadcast Equipment and Technology

"*Often I tape-recorded a player interview to use as my first-intermission feature, then interview a guest live during the second intermission. One game, I got the great idea that for my taped segment I would interview the Zamboni driver at the Pacific Coliseum, Eric Dickenson (he and his brother were great lacrosse players). For the interview, I sat beside Eric on the Zamboni while he cleaned the ice. I wanted to ask about the thickness of the ice and get a description of how to drive the Zamboni, but the machine was so noisy you could hardly hear the interview. I probably ran the tape on air, but I shouldn't have. It ended up being a brutal idea.*

"*Today the mikes are much better. Before the headset microphones, I worked with a yoke [a shoulder harness that held the microphone] and a pencil mike, which meant that I could hear all the sound around me. There was a natural tendency to shout when the crowd noise went up. By the late 1970s, I started to go hoarse. Luckily, the headset microphones came along and changed all that. They enabled me to hear myself and saved my voice.*

"*With the full headsets, your sound was in one ear and the TV director's was in the other. Having the director's feed bothered some people, but I always liked it. In the early years you could hear him talking to the cameras or sound guys, whereas in the later years the technology changed so you could only hear the director when he was talking to you.*

"*Once in the late 1970s we had a foul-up on dates at Denver's McNichols Arena. I got there, but the engineer never showed up. All I had was a telephone and a little Sony cassette machine that I used for interviews. I devised a way to put the brake on the Sony and set it on Record so it would act as an amplifier. Then I took the mouthpiece off the telephone, put two alligator clips on either side of the metal bar and plugged the other end into the cassette's jack. Then, by plugging a handheld microphone into the tape machine, I had a contraption that gave me an amplifier feeding a telephone. So I called the station, but I was worried about the batteries lasting in the cassette. Luckily, I had an AC adapter that I plugged into an outlet below. After the game, the Denver broadcaster came by and said, 'You plugged in down there? Those sockets are dead.' I had done the whole game on batteries. My contraption could have died on-air and I would never have known it.*"

● ● ● ●

PERIOD 1 2 3 OT TIMEOUT

SABRES magazine

FEBRUARY
FOES:

HARTFORD
VANCOUVER
PITTSBURGH
DETROIT
MONTREAL

the people's
choice

Fan Favorite Rob Ray

$3.00

ALSO INSIDE: Super Scout • Valuable Commodity • Sour Grapes

Excerpt of Jim (JR) and Harry's (HN) on-air banter from the second period of this BCTV/CKNW simulcast game. The exchange ends with Jim's much-loved "hello" to shut-ins.

HN: Well, McGeough was scraped along the boards when Colin Patterson fell into them and the puck was flipped up off the glass and hit him right in the head. He appears to be all right. He got a little bit of first aid from the Buffalo trainer and he's going to continue here.

JR: He's from Regina, Harry. / **HN:** Ah, they make 'em tough out there. He won't be as cute as he was before the game, but so what. He's doing a good job. Scapinello is phoning home to see if he can get some veal scallopini ready for him after the game [JR laughing in the background]. Ah, he must be phoning up to John D'Amico who's up there — he's the supervisor — telling John, "Don't run down to get dressed; McGeough's all right."

JR: Ray Scapinello is one of the league's more experienced linesmen. He worked last night with Leon Stickle, and I thought Ray was the senior man but he said no, Stickle's got one year on him. So Stickle had to referee the last period last night in Toronto. Garry Valk tips the puck into the Sabres zone but the play is offside. That was a two-line pass. At this time I'd like to pass along our usual hello to hospital patients and shut-ins, the pensioners, the blind. There are a lot of people that don't get out to hockey games but enjoy hockey and listen in to our broadcasts. We do appreciate you listening in tonight from Buffalo.

CBC Sports

PINNACLE

Harry NEALE

Soviet Snipers Turned Set-up Men
Vancouver Canucks @ Buffalo Sabres–February 12, 1993

The match was billed as a showdown between the two Russian superstars, Alexander Mogilny and Pavel Bure, a duo that had burst onto the hockey stage in 1989 as linemates of Sergei Fedorov at the World Junior Championships. At this point they were both in the midst of career seasons: Mogilny would end up with 76 goals and 51 assists, Bure with 60 goals and 50 helpers. But listeners in Vancouver were equally intrigued — and entertained — by the broadcast duo of Jim Robson and Harry Neale, a pairing necessitated by the absence of Jim's regular sidekick, the vacationing Tom Larscheid.

"Harry is such a quotable, colourful guy," Jim said. He fondly recalls trying to 'coach' Neale, then the Canucks' bench boss, on his media relations in the 1980s. "I would tell him, 'Harry, you can't say things like that. If they ever print that stuff, you'll be in real trouble.' But Harry would just scoff, 'They won't print it, because if they do I'll never give them anything again.' He was always media-savvy, and popular with the media."

Neale's capacity for frankness was on display after the Canucks lost at home to Montreal — a game in which the fans showed more support for the Habs than the home side. As Jim tells it, during the interview Harry steamed, "Vancouver fans are a**holes." Reminded he was on live radio, Neale shot back, "You're right. I shouldn't be calling those a**holes a**holes!"

Although this Buffalo game was his only broadcast with Harry Neale, Jim observes that "Harry really prepares for games. Because he is a very well read, smart guy, Harry always has a couple of lines prepared for each broadcast." On this night at the Memorial Auditorium, both the on-air and on-ice shows lived up to their billing. The spirited game ended 3–1 in favour of the Canucks, and both superstars created numerous scoring chances, assisting on each of their team's goals.

"One of my shticks before away games was to wait in the chute where the Zamboni® ice resurfacer would park and tape-record an interview with a player for the broadcast. Then, at the end of the Canucks' skate, I'd take a Canucks decal and I'd stick it on the side of the Zamboni® ice resurfacer opposite to the driver. Then during the intermissions I'd watch, and most nights it would still be on there during the game. One night in Buffalo, one of the guys working in the rink caught me putting the sticker on the Zamboni® ice resurfacer. He chewed me out and made me take it off. I must have stuck those stickers on more than 100 ice resurfacers, but that was the only time I got caught." — *JR*

Always ahead of his time, Jim's sticker caper was a precursor to the now-famous Canadian tradition of hiding a loonie (a Canadian one-dollar coin) under centre ice. Jim was also known to pose for family vacation pictures holding a Canucks sticker — most notably at the General Wolfe statue in Quebec City, atop Windermere Hill in England, and beside a Mozart monument in Salzburg, Austria.

© Zamboni Company

PERIOD 1 2 3 OT

VAN 3
BUF 1 F

37

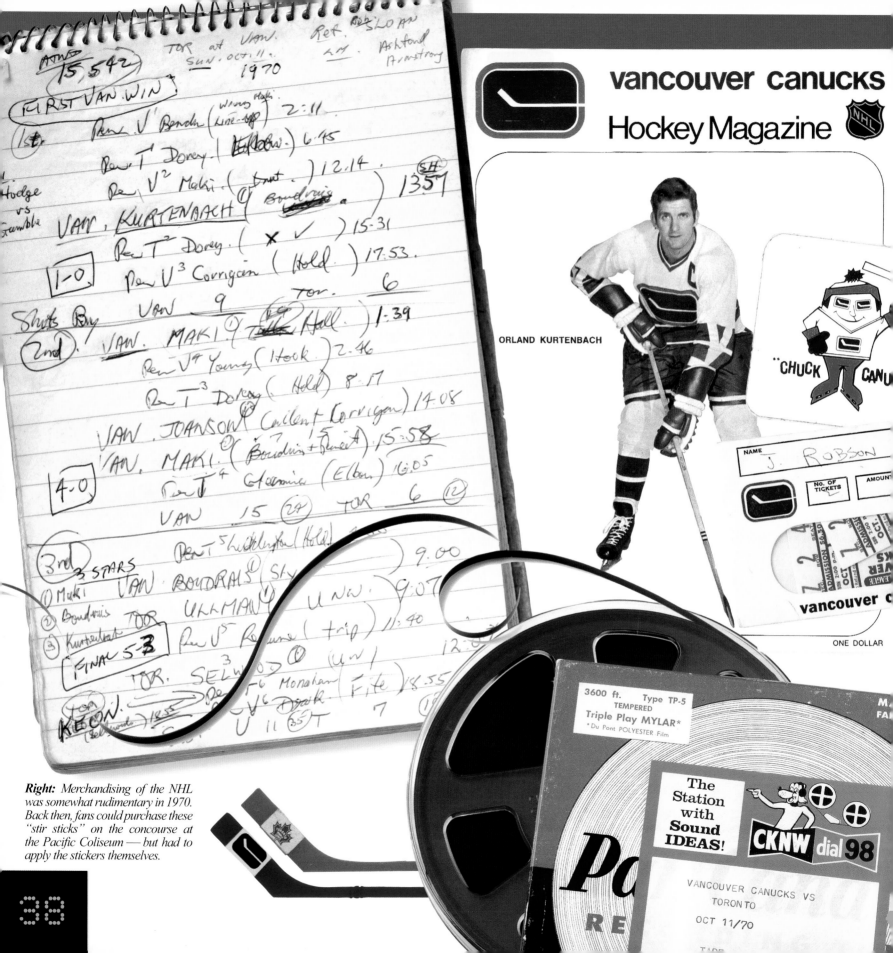

Right: *Merchandising of the NHL was somewhat rudimentary in 1970. Back then, fans could purchase these "stir sticks" on the concourse at the Pacific Coliseum — but had to apply the stickers themselves.*

On a Sunday afternoon in October 1970, hockey fans filed into the Pacific Coliseum to witness a bit of history. For the first time since the 1920s, an eastern pro team had ventured to Canada's Pacific coast for a meaningful game. Moreover, the match marked the first-ever regular-season NHL battle between teams from eastern and western Canada. The atmosphere was electric that afternoon, in part because of the Canucks' competitive — albeit losing — debut against L.A. two nights before, but largely because Vancouverites were eager to get their first glimpse of the Leafs, who for years had been rendered larger than life by national radio and TV coverage.

The 15,542 fans were treated to spirited hockey in the first period. Captain Canuck, Orland Kurtenbach, brought the crowd to its feet when he opened the scoring with the franchise's second-ever goal — and its first-ever shorthanded goal. Let's go to the booth and pick up Jim's call with Canucks' defenceman Darryl Sly gaining control of the puck.

"… Sly picks it up … Sly, ragging the puck out at centre, got away from one check … carries it back to his own line and gives it to Reaume. Reaume puts it across to Boudrias. Boudrias to Kurtenbach, by himself at centre with two men back. In on Lee on the right … Boudrias getting in front, and the puck is grabbed by the goaltender. Scramble — loose puck! Kurtenbach picks it up — open net. He scores! …

[Uninterrupted applause and horns for 20 seconds.] It's Vancouver one, Toronto nothing. Orland Kurtenbach hit an open net as Gamble had trouble controlling a goalmouth pass that Kurtenbach had thrown out for Boudrias, and the puck got away from Gamble. Kurtenbach picked it up, got out in front, and back-handed it into an open net while killing a penalty. …"

That goal, and two from number 11, Wayne Maki, in the second, was more than enough to give Canuck fans their first taste of big-league victory.

Here are a few pieces of news and notes related by CKNW radio personality Al Davidson during the game broadcast and on the White Spot Overtime Show:

On Saturday's out-of-town scoreboard, Gordie Howe recorded one goal and one assist playing as a defenceman in a 5–3 Detroit win over Oakland. Meanwhile, young Gil Perreault scored his first NHL goal.

The Canucks' first-ever draft pick, Dale Tallon, celebrated his 20th birthday.

The Leafs boasted new uniforms in 1970–71, upsetting some traditionalists.

Canucks defenceman Pat Quinn was scratched in favour of newly signed Howie Young. For the Leafs, Rick Ley (later coach of the Canucks and a Leafs assistant coach) played for Toronto, and rookie Darryl Sittler dressed, although he didn't play much.

Leafs defenceman Brad Selwood made his NHL debut and scored his first career goal. He was no stranger to Canucks fans, having won Rookie of the Year honours with the WHL Canucks the previous year.

"When the NHL came to Vancouver, CBC wanted the TV cameras on the west side of the Pacific Coliseum, so the radio was moved to the east side. It ended up being a very good broadcast location. I liked looking into the benches. Although I leaned forward if the play went down into the right-hand corner, there were no blind spots from my booth and I could see everything well." —JR

"Al Davidson had a terrific voice, great pipes. He sat in with me at home games during the first year, made the odd comment on the broadcast, and ran downstairs to do press-room interviews during intermissions. Al was a big booster of mine. But it wasn't always that way. On CKNW, Al used to call me the 'Bush Leaguer on Burrard' when I worked at CKWX. The rivalry between the stations was so intense that once when I ran into Al with his 12-year-old son, the boy waited until his dad wasn't looking and whispered to me, 'I listen to you call Mounties baseball on CKWX but don't tell my Dad.' Al was a character, truly unique." —JR

VANCOUVER

PERIOD 1 2 3 OT

TOR 3
VAN 5

F

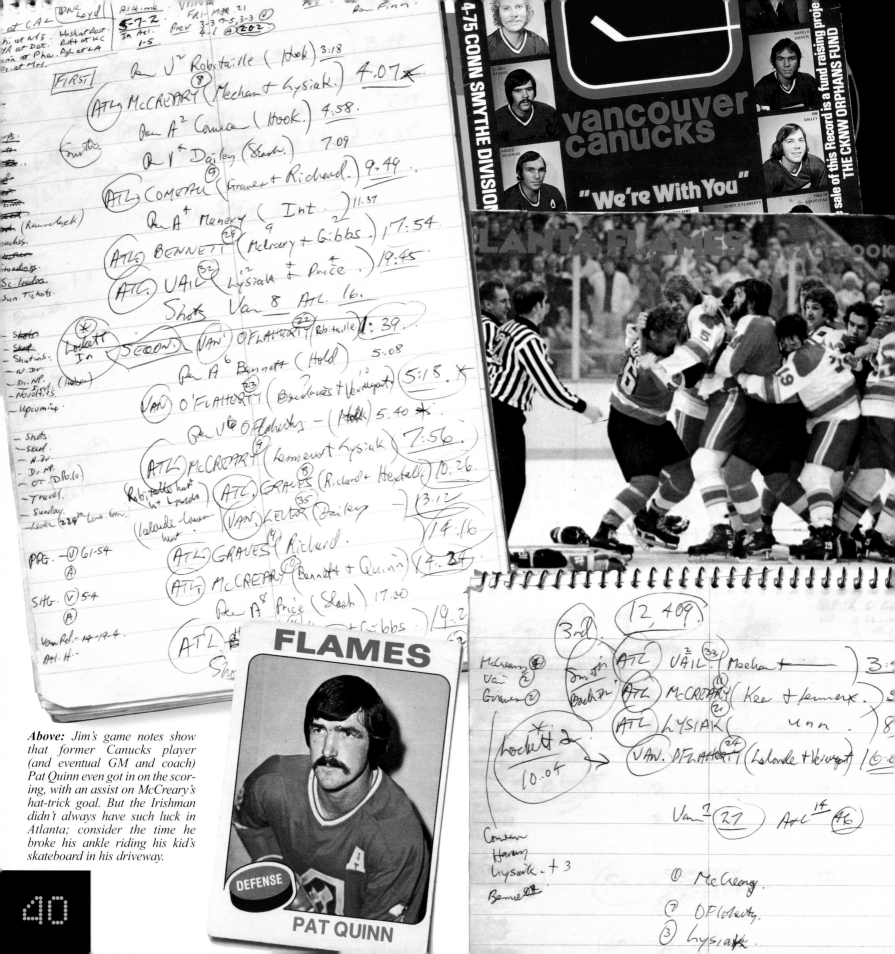

Above: *Jim's game notes show that former Canucks player (and eventual GM and coach) Pat Quinn even got in on the scoring, with an assist on McCreary's hat-trick goal. But the Irishman didn't always have such luck in Atlanta; consider the time he broke his ankle riding his kid's skateboard in his driveway.*

With the regular season winding down, Canucks coach Phil Maloney was concerned that some of his players were getting too comfortable with the team's first-place standing. Taking a page out of Flyers coach Fred Shero's book of mind games, Maloney called a team meeting in his hotel room for 11 p.m. the night before the game. Anxious to bring about a change in the players' attitude, he was also hoping for a change of behaviour — or, as he put it, "Maybe after the meeting some of the guys will decide to go to bed early." The team didn't improve on either count. Instead, they fell behind 4–0 after one period and 9–3 after two, eventually losing 12–4. To that date, no Canucks team had ever allowed as many goals (see Edmonton, pages 52–53), and the total of 16 was a high-water mark for an NHL game at The Omni.

Seven of the Flames' goals were scored against Gary Smith, who was replaced by Ken Lockett in the second. Smith returned for the third, before Lockett again relieved him. Meanwhile the performance up front was no better. Just ask right winger Gerry O'Flaherty, who notched a hat trick but still finished the night minus-1. It seems he forgot to check the winger he was matched against, Keith McCreary, who scored four of his own. McCreary's scoring outburst vaulted his season total to 11 goals. His fourth tally wound up being his last goal of his workmanlike 532-game NHL career.

Intentional or not, Keith's offensive attack on this night exacted some family

revenge on the Canucks. The year before, Keith's older brother Bill McCreary (Sr.) had been fired as head coach of the Canucks. While that termination may have surprised the McCreary clan, it was the hiring of Bill McCreary that surprised Jim Robson. "I went on the air and speculated that Al Arbour would be the next Canucks coach," admits Jim. "But after Arbour met with Coley Hall and the other Canuck owners, he backed out because he didn't like the set-up. Bill Sr. was waiting in the wings, having played for the Springfield Indians in the American league, who were coached by Coley Hall's buddy, Eddie Shore. Hall didn't have much of the action, but he had a big say in how the Canucks were run in those days, and so he went with Shore's guy."

The friendly endorsement didn't endure long. Forty-one games into the 1973–74 season, McCreary was fired and replaced by Phil Maloney. Maloney's failed coaching experiment on the eve of the Atlanta scorching probably led him to contemplate whether ownership might have any late-season surprises in store for him, too.

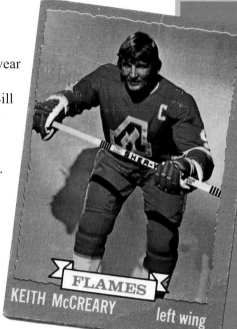

KEITH McCREARY — FLAMES — left wing

"The outside of the Omni was a strange, multi-sided shape with an unusual copper colouring, kind of like rusty steel. Inside, the ice seemed to be at an angle to the building. Atlanta crowds were enthusiastic and always had a lot of attractive southern belles." — *JR*

"On one visit, my colour man, Tom Larscheid, got a gift certificate for three pairs of free shoes. Tom said to me, 'C'mon, this will be great.' I said 'Naw, I remember getting the same thing one time in Philadelphia and I couldn't find three pairs that I wanted in the whole place.' Nonetheless, he went to the store and was so proud of his new shoes. Of course, in the first rainstorm they disintegrated. The soles were pulp and as soon as they got wet all the glue came out and he was walking around in cardboard. I still tease him: 'Any more deals on Atlanta shoes, Tom?' " — *JR*

ATLANTA

PHA at NYI.
SAT. May. 24/80
GAME 6. ST. CUP FINAL
Prev. 4-3 (OT) 3-8, 6-2, 5-2, 3-4
Hill me by. 18-20-8 Reg. S.(2-2)
Pen Pch: 1

Ref: Copetown
NYI: Ron Finn
11th yr. TOR
Leon Stickle
10th yr. — TOR
Standby Ref:
minor off — Boston
S/B A.V. Hellerud.

Goal: Peeters (8-4) 2.62
Series: 2-2.
Season: (29-5-5) 2.73

SMITH (14-4) 2.76 20th gm
Series: 3-2.
Season: 15-14-7. 2.85

FIRST

Pen P 2 Holmgren (Hi StK) 1:00
Pen NYI Lane (") "
Pen P 4 Dupont (Ai StK) 2.24
Pen P 9 Kelly (5-Fite) 5.55
Pen NYI 9 Nystrom (5 Fite) "
Pen NYI 11 Potvin (XV) 6.24
PHA. LEACH (McIlhish & Barber) 7.4
Pen P 11 Holmgren (Hook.) 7:42
Pen P 13 Linseman (D. Goal) 8.11
Pen NYI 13 Bourne (") "
Pen P 15 Busnik (Hold) 10.15.
NYI POTVIN (Bossy + Trottier) 11.56 *
NYI D. SUTTER (Gillies + Goring) 14.08.
Pen P 27 Bridgman Rough 15:18.
Pen NYI 25 Nystrom (") "
Pen P 29 Dupont (Hold) 16.25
PHA PROPP (Holmgren + Linseman) 18.58

Pen P 6 — NY 13

SECOND

Pen P 31 Watson (Rough) 3:15
Pen NYI 27 Howatt (") "
Pen P 33 Wilson (Hold.) 6:39
NYI BOSSY (Persson + Bourne) 7
Pen P 35 McIlhargey (Hook) 8:4
Pen P 37 Ni. Olgson (Rough) 11:10
Pen NYI 29 Bossy (Hi StK) "
Pen P 4 Dupont (2 Rough) 14.2
Pen NYI 37 Tonelli (Slash) "
Pen P 43 Linseman (Abuse) 15:0
Pen NYI 33 Potvin (") "
NYI NYSTROM (Tonelli) —
Shots Pha 6 NY 12
THIRD
PHA DAILEY (Linseman + Holmgren) 1:
Pen NYI 33 Nystrom (Hold.) 3.
PHA PADDOCK (Dupont + McIlhish)
Pen P 50 Holmgren (XV + Knee)
Pen NYI 40 Gillies (Slash + Fite)
Pen P 52 Linseman (Rough.)

OT
NYI NYSTROM Tonelli 7:11

NYI 5 Ph. 4
NYI win Cup Final 4 gms-2.

❝ *…on the stick of Tonelli. Coming in with Nystrom. Tonelli to Nystrom…he scores! Bob Nystrom scores the goal! The Islanders win the Stanley Cup!*" And so a hard-fought six-game series ended in dramatic fashion. For Hockey Night in Canada viewers from coast to coast, Jim's famous call of the drama on Long Island almost didn't come to be.

"For the first five games of the 1980 Cup finals," Jim starts in, "the network rights holders, USA TV and CBC, got together and decided to share the audio broadcasts. That meant that I got to share the play-by-play with [the St. Louis Blues' Hall of Fame broadcaster] Dan Kelly, which was great because he was a long-time friend. I did half the game, and in the middle of the second period I'd introduce Dan. Then next game, Dan would start and halfway through the second period he'd give me a big flowery introduction and I'd pick up the call. I don't think that's been done since and I don't think it'll be done again.

"Dan's stock was so high that he could have demanded to do the whole games, but he didn't. Instead he and I, along with HNiC producer John Shannon, had a great time driving between Philadelphia and Long Island, swapping old sports broadcasting stories. For game six, CBS had the U.S. rights and decided to air the game coast to coast, which was a huge deal for the NHL. As a result, I got to call the entire game, and Nystrom's famous goal, for CBC across Canada."

Nystrom's goal, his flowing hair, his jump into the corner boards and the pure joy of his teammates mobbing him are all etched indelibly in the memories of hockey fans who saw the game. Nystrom's historic marker was his second of the game and the fourth of his career in overtime (at the time, second all-time after Maurice Richard's six). To a new generation of fans, Nystrom instantly symbolized the big-game player. But his "do what it takes to win" attitude might have rendered him unavailable to finish the game. In the first period he fought Bob "Hound Dog" Kelly, and in the second he and Mel Bridgman were each given 10-minute misconducts to go along with roughing minors. Nystrom's aggression in such a crucial game was a rarity. Since then, there has only been one fight in a Cup-deciding game — in 1985. But Nystrom did finish game six against the Flyers — literally. Quipped Nystrom, "The thing that makes overtime so great is that you can score the goal and leave." Nystrom's big-game reputation was reinforced the next spring, when he assisted on the Islanders' second-ever Cup-winning goal.

"CBC had a really good crew of technical people, including two great cameramen that they sent in from Toronto especially for the finals on Long Island. CBC really knew what they were doing on hockey — gee, they were good. So good, in fact, that I remember another network's cameraman even taped a wire along the top of the boards to his position so he could listen to CBC's audio because he didn't want to be directed by the Americans." — *JR*

"I liked Nassau Coliseum in the early years, before they built the broadcast press box. Even though they put us in the back row of seats, quite often the Islander players who did not dress would sit next to me and my engineer. I really liked that, because the guy sitting there isn't with your team and he got to hear the job I did. That's a good incentive to do a good, balanced job because I wanted to show them I wasn't a 'homer.' I also liked having players nearby so they would get an idea of what it's like to broadcast the game they play." — *JR*

LONG ISLAND

PERIOD 1 2 3 OT

PHI	4	
NYI	5	**F OT**

(NYI win best-of-7 Cup Final, 4–2)

KANSAS C...
MEDIA GUIDE
1975-76 $1.00

SCOUTS — SMYTHE DIVISION
Team transferred to Colorado.

Above: Wilf Paiement pictured with Ed Gilbert celebrating a rare KC goal. Soon after Wayne Gretzky made sweater #99 famous, Wilf Paiement then with Toronto, followed suit. But in his days with Kansas City and Colorado, Paiement wore the more traditional #9.

Right: In the second period, Scouts centreman Henry Boucha got KC on the board with his second-to-last goal of the season, and of his career. Boucha holds the distinction of being the first NHL skater to wear a headband in an NHL game. Perhaps coincidentally, he missed most of the 1975–76 season due to a head injury.

Bottom right: Jim's game notes show that Craig Patrick scored shorthanded in the third to make things interesting. Patrick later followed in his family's footsteps, becoming coach and GM of the Rangers in the 1980s, after which he guided the Penguins to two Cups as GM in the early 1990s.

ROCKIES
Team transferred to Colorado.
HENRY BOUCHA • CENTER

44

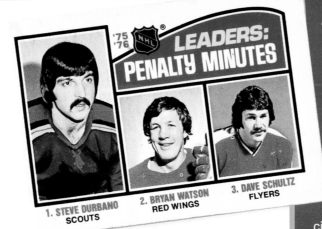

LEADERS: PENALTY MINUTES

1. STEVE DURBANO SCOUTS
2. BRYAN WATSON RED WINGS
3. DAVE SCHULTZ FLYERS

In their musical *Oklahoma!*, Rodgers and Hammerstein wrote that "Everything's up to date in Kansas City," but as the Canucks took the ice at the Kemper Arena for the last time, their thoughts were anything but lyrical. They had lost their two previous matches in the Missouri cowtown, and ended up with only a 2–3–1 record during the Scouts' two-year existence. As Canucks coach Phil Maloney put it at the time, "I'd just like to wash this place from my mind. It seems we can play great against teams like Montreal, Buffalo and Philadelphia and come up with duds against last-place clubs" like the Scouts. But the Canucks came up with a good effort on this night. They jumped out to a 3–0 first-period lead, highlighted by Don Lever's 20th goal of the season.

That goal came on a Canucks' power play — in fact, only 17 seconds before they were enjoying a two-man advantage. The penalized Scout who had just returned to the ice was no stranger to the box. Steve Durbano led the league in penalty minutes that season, with 369. In an era marred by goon hockey, Durbano was in a class by himself. Take for example 1974–75, when he only played in one game but managed to draw 10 PIM. Over his 220-game NHL career, he averaged more than five minutes per game in penalties — a higher rate than any of the top 10 career penalty-minute leaders. Even Tiger Williams spent "only" 4:07 in the sin bin during an average game.

True to form, Durbano was in a surly mood against the Canucks this night, starting with a first-period slashing penalty, another of the same in the second, two for high-sticking in the third, and then seven minutes for fighting Mike Walton (and Harold Snepsts, the third man in).

Durbano's antics helped Vancouver to a 5–3 win; in fact, the Canucks put together back-to-back wins that weekend, en route to a season-ending run of 8–5–2. However, they suffered a quick playoff exit: the Islanders swept them in two games in the preliminary round. The Scouts, meanwhile, finished the season 0–21–6, landing them in last place with an awful record of 12–56–12 overall. Not surprisingly, the Scouts struggled to draw fans, forcing their 37 investors, who were almost a million dollars in debt, to initiate a ticket drive during the 1975–76 season. Setting a goal of 8,000 subscribers, the Scouts sold only a quarter of that number, and concluded that hockey would not work in Kansas City. That conclusion no doubt suited Phil Maloney just fine, for after the win Maloney could wash his mind — and travel itinerary— of Kansas City.

"In Kansas City we stayed at a Holiday Inn downtown with a restaurant on the top. Before the game, I had a disappointing steak up there. The TV guys told us it was corn-fed, and we're used to grain-fed, which tastes better. I also went to a jazz club there one night — not many other places on the NHL circuit where you could hear Dixieland." — *JR*

"The hockey team was very poor and wore gosh-awful uniforms. The Kemper Arena was a conventional two-level rink, like the Pacific Coliseum, with a walkway all around at each level. Inside it was dull, as the seats were all blue. Although the arena was downtown, the building was never full. Hockey never did go over well there." Jim was right: the Scouts averaged only 7,354 on the six occasions they hosted the Canucks. — *JR*

"The Scouts' media guides all boasted of talent which never materialized. Perhaps their coach, Bep Guidolin, should have dusted off his skates. After all, he played in the NHL at age 16 — the youngest ever NHL player." — *JR*

KANSAS CITY

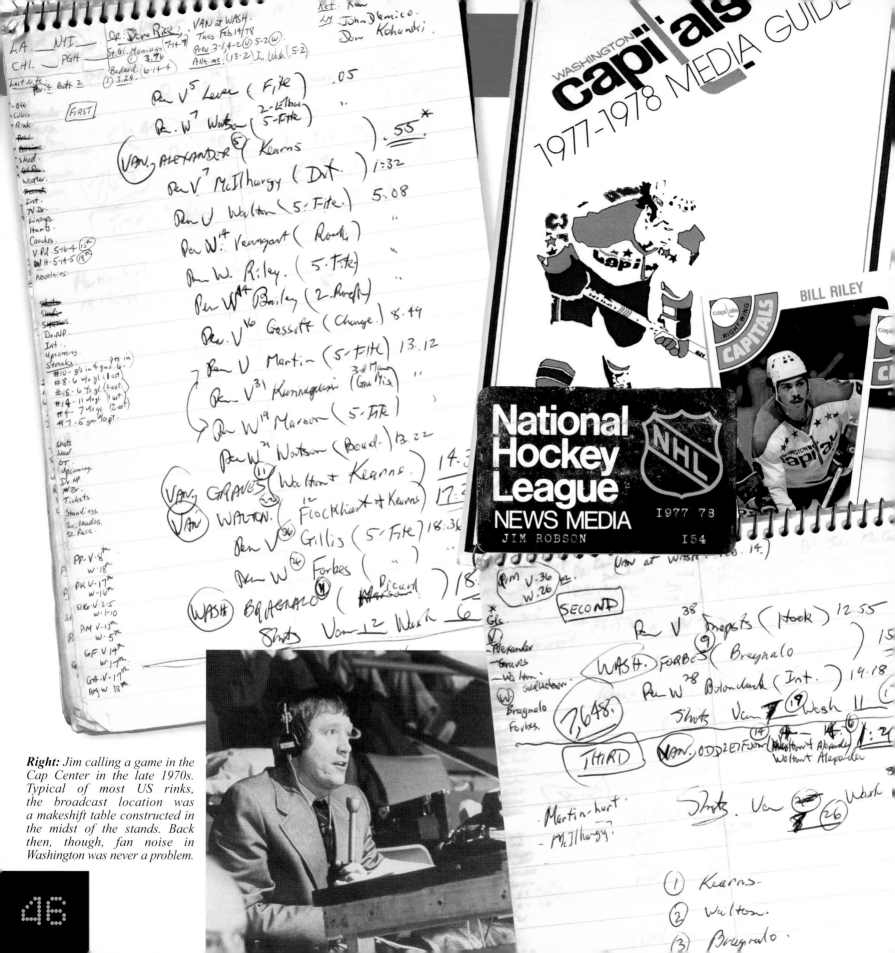

Right: Jim calling a game in the Cap Center in the late 1970s. Typical of most US rinks, the broadcast location was a makeshift table constructed in the midst of the stands. Back then, though, fan noise in Washington was never a problem.

If you were a team in a slump in the 1970s, the best cure was a date with the Washington Capitals. And so it was in February 1978 for the Canucks — losers of 5 straight and with only 4 wins in their previous 26 outings. After the last game, an 8–3 loss in Detroit, captain Don Lever had ripped into his teammates: "Ten guys had no guts…they should be ashamed of themselves." But the schedule-maker must have had a soft spot in his heart for the Canucks that Valentine's Day as he paired them with the cellar-dwelling Caps.

Before the game, Lever convened a 90-minute players-only meeting. "I don't know about those player meetings," said Gary Smith, the former Canucks goalie now serving a tour with Washington. "We lead the league in them, and look where we are in the standings." One of those who attended the session felt it was just what the relationship doctor ordered. "We got a lot of things off our chests in that meeting," said defenceman Dennis Kearns. "There was a lot of constructive criticism."

While the Canucks may have been feeling warm and fuzzy by the opening face-off, the Caps from the outset were in anything but a loving mood. Career linesman John D'Amico and youngster Don Koharski, who would become better known as a referee, had their hands full, breaking up four first-period fights and another in the second. Admirably,

the Canucks had guts on this night; the four who answered the bell were not known as fighters, averaging less than 40 penalty minutes that season. Conversely, the Capital combatants — Bryan Watson, Bill Riley, Mike Marson and Dave Forbes — were no strangers to fisticuffs: all amassed more than 100 penalty minutes.

1976–77 Royal Leaders

PLAYER OF THE WEEK

The fights, however, took their toll. Four Canucks needed x-rays after the game. Three had to leave in the first period: Jack McIlhargey (ribs); Pit Martin (shoulder), who was shaken like a rag doll by his much larger dance partner Mike Marson; and Sheldon Kannegiesser, who was tossed for trying to cut in on the Martin/Marson tango. Vancouver was down to four defencemen, led by the rejuvenated Dennis Kearns, who took control of the play with his puck handling en route to two power-play goals.

Centre Mike Walton then scored the eventual game winner to make it 3–0 late in the first period. Walton's goal completed his "Gordie Howe hat trick" — a goal, an assist and a fight — and it only took him until 17:28 of the first period. The rare trick was enough to land Walton the second star in a game not in keeping with the spirit of St. Valentine. It was fitting then that both teams were without tickets to the post-season ball.

"The Capital Center was a big, very dark rink in Landover, Maryland. It was located on a freeway called the Beltway between Baltimore and Washington, way out in the middle of nowhere. It was an isolated place with no facilities around it, so we always had to stay a bus ride away." — *JR*

"One time we stayed at a Marriott in Arlington, Virginia, that looked across at the Washington Monument. It was a Friday-night game and the team bus didn't show up, so they got taxis for all the players, four to a cab. I got into a cab with colour man Garry Monahan and the Canuck coaches, Roger Neilson and Ron Smith. Friday traffic out of Washington was horrendous and our cabbie was hopeless. We arrived at the rink while the players were on the ice for the pregame warmup. Luckily we had a good engineer in Washington who had the equipment set up. But with less than five minutes to air time we still scrambled to call the station and start the broadcast." — *JR*

WASHINGTON

IM BEDARD

W ild: Broad Street Bullies Court Disaster

Philadelphia Flyers 4 @ Vancouver Canucks 4 — December 29, 1972

Once the last of the eight goals had been scored in this game, all that remained was to settle a few scores on the ice. One Vancouver fan in Section F of the Pacific Coliseum tried to lend the homeside a hand, and in so doing caused a near-riot in the stands. With Canucks rookie and hometown boy Barry Wilcox in trouble against his bigger Flyers adversary Don Saleski, an unidentified fan reached over the glass and grabbed hold of the hair on Saleski's helmetless head. That prompted a posse of Flyers, led by backup goalie Bobby Taylor, to scale the glass. Newspaper accounts of the incident stated that "there were as many as a dozen Flyers in the aisles, flailing away at everybody in sight with their sticks." Taylor was accused of knocking down a police corporal who tried to intervene. Taylor's take on the incident was simple: "Those fans are nuts in this town. . . . No way I punched that cop." The wild incident ended up in court, and three Flyer players — including Taylor — ultimately received suspended sentences and paid fines. The court appearance coincided with the Flyers' next game in Vancouver, on February 9, 1973. No one knows if the fan who started the incident was on hand that night to see the Flyers exact revenge in a 10–5 drubbing of the Canucks.

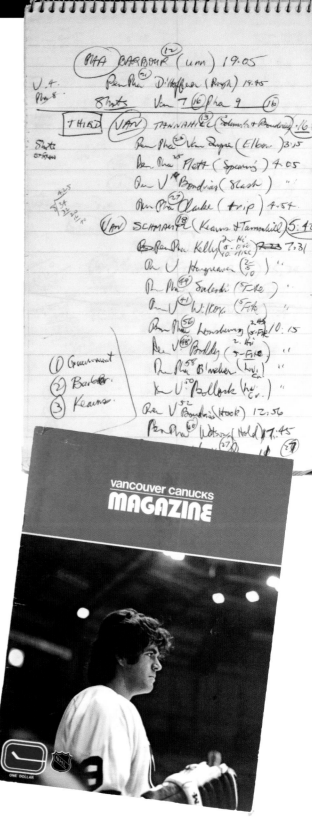

Weird: Canucks and Rangers on their Best Behaviour

New York Rangers 7 @ Vancouver Canucks 3 — March 13, 1976

Referee Lloyd Gilmour, prominently wearing jersey number 45, was the least prominent person on the ice this night. After blowing his whistle to summon the starting centres for the opening face-off, he didn't use it again. Throughout 60 minutes of NHL hockey, not one infraction of the rules caught his eye.

Without a doubt, the player who benefited most from the display of gentlemanly conduct was the Rangers' 20-year-old rookie, Wayne Dillon, who racked up a mere 10 minutes in penalties in 79 games that season. Dillon — chosen 13th overall in the draft, ahead of fellow centres Pierre Mondou, Tim Young, Dennis Maruk and Doug Jarvis — happily found lots of open ice from which to score his first NHL hat trick (of two in his career). Dillon's career soon fizzled — he would score only 43 goals in his entire NHL career — a far cry from the totals of 194, 195, 356 and 139 registered by the others respectively. But it's likely that none of them played in a penalty-free NHL game.

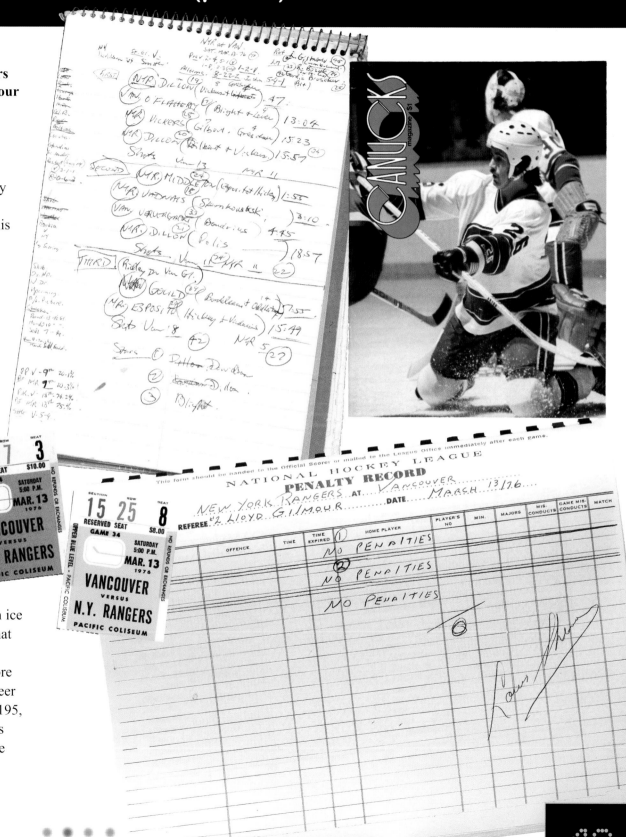

3rd pe

COMMENT TO ON

"STAND BY FOR THE 1

COMMERCIAL - CLIENT

COMMERCIAL - CLIENT

COMMERCIAL - CLIENT

Play-by-play...thre

commercials inserte

"THE SCORE...THIS I

COMMERCIAL - CLIENT

"THE SCORE...MORE H

COMMERCIAL - CLIENT

"THE SCORE....FROM

COMMERCIAL - CLIENT

...MORE C

- CLIENT

- CLIENT

THE FINAL

Y IN A MOM

IAL - CLIEN

IAL - CLIENT   CART #

and comment to:-

NAL SCORE AGAIN...THIS IS JIM ROBSON/COX/HUGHS

city)____. (pause) STAND BY FOR OUR POST-GAME

OVERTIME".

CIAL - CLIENT   CART #

CIAL - CLIENT   CART #

IGN-OFF

RCIAL-CLIENT   CART #
46:    30 SEC: RCIAL - CLIENT   CART #
47:    30 SEC: COMMERCIAL - CLIENT   CART #

N E W S H E A D L I N E S (2:30)

Above: *Pomp and ceremony: Jim presents the Fred 'Cyclone' Taylor Award to Canucks player-of-the-year "King Richard" Brodeur in 1982 . . .*

Right: *. . . and to Stan Smyl in 1981.*

Schedule of Memorable Nights

OCTOBER

		1	2	3	4	5
PIT/FLA 6 76 / '00	7	8	DET 9 1995	BOS 10 1973	TOR 11 1970	12
	EDM 14 1979	15	16	17	18	19
20	21	22	23	24	25	26
TOR 27 1971	28	29	30	PHO 31 2003		

NOVEMBER

					1	2
3	4	5	6	7	EDM 8 1985	9
10	QUE/MIN 11 '89 / '01	12	13	NJ 14 1996	15	16
MIN 17 1988	18	19	20	21	DAL/ATL 22 '95 / '99	23
STL 24 1990	NYR 25 1997	26	CAR 27 2002	28		30

HOME year   AWAY year

JIM ROBSON

" what a difference a voice makes"

CEMBER

	2	3	4	5	6	7
A 9	9	**TOR** 10 1980	11	12	13	14
	16	17	18	19	20	21
	23	24	25	26		**SJ** 28 1991
IL 2	30	31				

NUARY

		BOS 1 1973	2	3	**COL** 4 1980	
	6	**MTL** 7 1987	8	9	10	11
	13	14	15	**PROV** 16 1968	17	18
H 9	**WPG** 20 1984	21	22	23	**DET** 24 1971	25
	27	28	29	30	31	

Western Hockey League

BRUARY

						1
	3	4	5	6	7	**All Star** 8 1983
	10	**DET** 11 1982	**BUF/TB** 12 '93 / '94	13	**WASH** 14 1978	15
L 04	**CLEV** 17 1978	18	19	20	**BOS** 21 2000	22
	24	25	26	27	28	

MARCH

		OAK 3 <TML>		5		1
		HART 3 1985		5	**KC CBJ** 6 '76 / '03	7	8
	9	10	11	12	**NYI** 13 1976	14	15
	16	17	18	19	20	**ATL** 21 1975	22
	LA 23 1994	24	25	26	27	28	29
	30	31				

APRIL

			1	2		**OTT** 4 1993	
	6	7	8	9	**PHIL** 10 1979	11	12
	13	**CAL** 14 1999	**MON** 15 1975	16	17	18	19
	20	**CAL** 21 <EDM> 1988	22	23	24	25	26
	27	28	**CHI** 29 1982	30			

<EDM> Edmonton at Calgary, "Battle of Alberta" classic

MAY

				1	2	3
	4	5	6	7	**NYI** 8 1982	9	10
	11	12	13	14	15	16	17
	18	19	20	21	22	23	**NYI** 24 <PHIL> 1980
	25	26	**BUF/CHI** 27 <PHIL> '75 / '95	28	29	30	31

<PHIL> Philadelphia at Buffalo Sabres, 1975

JUNE

1	2	3	4	5	6	7
8	9	10	**NYR** 11 1994	12	13	14
15	16	17	18	19	20	21
22	23	24	25	26	27	28
29	30					

HOCKEY PLAY-BY-PLAY
Around the NHL with Jim Robson

> " *My first hockey broadcast was an intermediate hockey game between the Lake Cowichan Bruins and the Alberni Valley Flyers on a Sunday morning in 1954 at the Nanaimo Civic Arena [on Vancouver Island]. I taped the game and drove the tape to CJAV radio station in Port Alberni so it could be aired that afternoon.* "

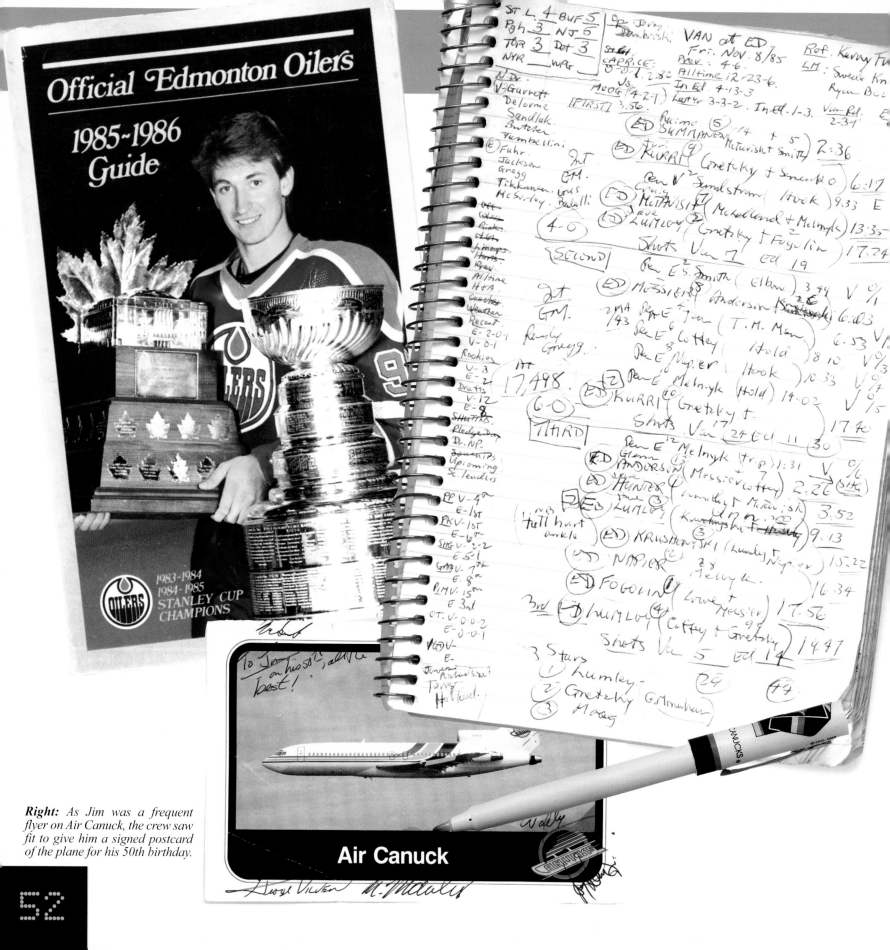

Right: As Jim was a frequent flyer on Air Canuck, the crew saw fit to give him a signed postcard of the plane for his 50th birthday.

Air Canuck

Sometimes a mismatch on paper doesn't translate into one on the ice. Intangibles like teamwork, effort and coaching can transform the whole into more than the sum of the parts. No such luck on this night: the game went according to expectations, and then some.

At 2:36 of the first period, Raimo Summanen of the Stanley Cup champion Oilers scored to open the floodgates against the Canucks and their beleaguered goalie, Frank Caprice. Edmonton went on to score three more in the first, then kill off five penalties and score two more in the second, before going for the jugular in the third with seven unanswered goals. Final tally: Oilers 13, Canucks 0. The game came close to equalling the most lopsided shutout in modern NHL history: a record set on January 23, 1944, when the Rangers lost 15–0 in Detroit. Looking back on that game, and era, of Oiler dominance over the Canucks, Robson quipped, "If we had had stress leave in some of those years, I would have taken it."

Recalling Canucks bench boss Tom Watt, Jim says, "He was a friendly guy, nice to talk to, but he wasn't prepared. It was amazing: Watt never did any homework. He'd say, 'Ah, I just worry about our team.'" Never was his approach more in evidence than this night. Surprisingly, the Oilers' usual suspects (Wayne Gretzky, Mark Messier, Jari Kurri, Glenn Anderson and Paul Coffey) played supporting roles, combining to score only four goals. Meanwhile, the team's plumbers (Dave Lumley, Dave Hunter, Craig MacTavish, Mike Krushelnyski, Lee Fogolin) got the opportunity to pad their stats.

As Jim notes, "The only Canuck penalty was Sundstrom, for hooking. Nobody got mad — no spunk. It really tells you something about the character of the team." The team's character might have been boosted if third-year player and eventual Hall of Famer Cam Neely wasn't perpetually benched. But Watt preferred Dave Lowry to Neely. As Jim tells it, "Watt would say, 'Lowry is twice the player that Neely is.' He played Lowry on the power play and put Cam on the fourth line. I don't know what Cam ever did to Tom."

Maintaining his laissez-faire attitude, Watt told his players not to dwell on the shellacking. To his credit, the Canucks bounced back with a 7–2 win the next night in Winnipeg. It was Watt's first time coaching there since being fired as Jets coach in 1983, in part because of the friction between Watt and Jets captain Dale Hawerchuck. On one occasion, Watt put his 1982 Coach-of-the-Year trophy in Hawerchuk's dressing-room stall to arrogantly remind him who was boss. Had Watt done his homework and been "worrying about his own team" at the time, he would have realized that his captain's 103-point season probably had a lot to do with his receiving the award in the first place.

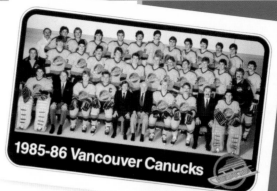

1985-86 Vancouver Canucks

"Edmonton was a pretty good place to work, and we always had good meals in the press room. Northlands Coliseum is based on the same design concept, called a drum style, as Vancouver's Pacific Coliseum, but larger." — *JR*

"Jerry Dombrowski was a great young radio engineer in Edmonton. He'd help me and get things like the out-of-town scores, the goal scorers, and other stats. He was a real hockey fan. Even though he was an Oilers fan he would do everything to help visiting radio during their broadcast, which really added to it and made it a pleasure to work there." — *JR*

"I used to tease Oilers play-by-play man Rod Philips about his calls of #99. He'd always be calling 'Gretzkeeeeeey.' Rod is such a good guy that we'd just laugh about it." — *JR*

EDMONTON

PERIOD 1 2 3 OT

VAN 0
EDM 13 F

53

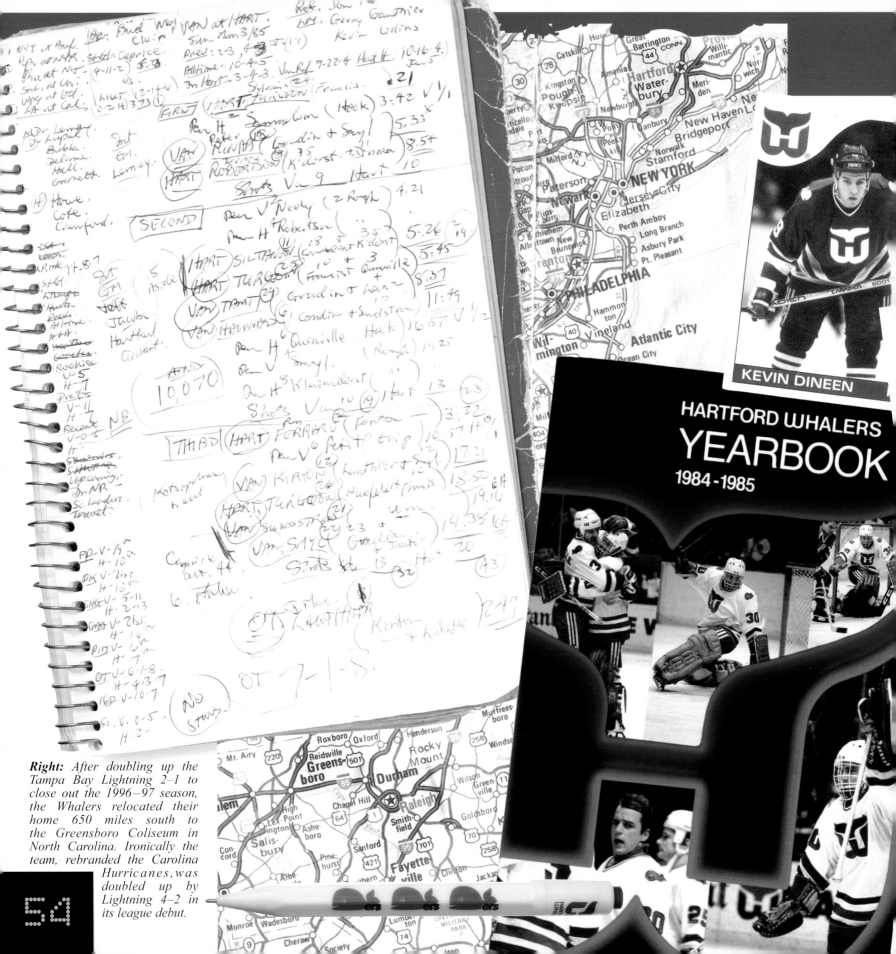

Right: *After doubling up the Tampa Bay Lightning 2–1 to close out the 1996–97 season, the Whalers relocated their home 650 miles south to the Greensboro Coliseum in North Carolina. Ironically the team, rebranded the Carolina Hurricanes, was doubled up by Lightning 4–2 in its league debut.*

KEVIN DINEEN

HARTFORD WHALERS
YEARBOOK
1984-1985

Twenty-one seconds after the puck dropped, Ron Francis fed Sylvain Turgeon for the opening goal and the Canucks saw first hand that the young Whalers were a team on the rise. Both Turgeon, age 20, and Francis, 22, were top-five draft picks and, despite their youth, had logged considerable time in the league. In 1984–85, the duo would be joined by three rookies, also Whaler draftees, who would go on to play more than 1,000 NHL games: Kevin Dineen, Ray Ferraro and Ulf Samuelson.

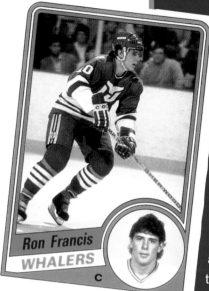

The Whalers still needed an all-important piece of the puzzle — goaltending! Ten days before hosting the Canucks, they acquired lanky All-Star netminder Mike Liut from the St. Louis Blues. After losing his first two games behind his new mates, Liut's frustration level was understandably running high. And by the time this game was over, it would boil over.

The game's early goal was the first of many in this high-scoring affair. The Francis-to-Turgeon connection clicked again in the second to put Hartford up 4–1. The Canucks, to their credit, kept battling; but at 18:50 of the third, it seemed futile. Turgeon — yes, with an assist from Francis — completed his hat trick, apparently sealing a 6–4 victory. Jim recalls clearly: "After Turgeon's last goal, most of the 10,070 made their way to the exits." After all, teams don't overcome two-goal deficits on the road with only 70 ticks left on the clock.

Canucks coach Harry Neale ordered goalie Frank Caprice off the ice for an extra attacker. The six Vancouver skaters controlled the play from the face-off, and at 19:16 Patrik Sundstrom struck to make it a one-goal game. Neale kept Caprice on the bench; the teams lined up at centre and, after another frantic 22 seconds of play, captain Stan Smyl miraculously scored to send the game into overtime. In the extra frame, unlikely hero Jean-Marc Lanthier iced the amazing come-from-behind win. "I had never seen a team score twice with the extra attacker," says Jim, "and I never saw it happen again."

After the game, Liut was furious and smashed his stick. But he and the other young Whalers would rebound from the collapse against the Canucks and become a solid regular-season team in the late 1980s. Still, in seven tries, Hartford never did oust their Adams Division rivals, the Bruins and Canadiens, from the playoffs.

"Hartford had some good hockey tradition from the old World Hockey Association days. Back then the team was known as the New England Whalers, Harry Neale coached, and the Howes, Dave Keon and Ricky Ley starred on the ice. While the teams were good and there was lots of hockey interest — particularly prep school and college hockey — the economy was not always great and so the move to Carolina was somewhat inevitable." — *JR*

"When you walked out of the arena at the Hartford Civic Center you found yourself in a mall boasting 145 shops — the problem was that 144 of them were out of business!" — *JR*

"Before the Canucks' run to the 1982 finals, we'd never seen their sweater being worn by fans in opposing rinks. But everywhere we went around the NHL for the next few years we saw their infamous 'V' sweater. A uniform can be the worst in the world, but if it's a successful team, fans will buy and wear the jersey." — *JR*

HARTFORD

PERIOD 1 2 3 OT

VAN	7	
HART	6	F OT

LE MEILLEUR

EST À VENIR

Media guide: *Québec's lame-looking media guide reflected the on-ice product. The hapless Nordiques ended dead last in the NHL in 1989–90 (going 12–61–7) for the second of three consecutive years — netting them three straight first-overall draft picks: Mats Sundin (1989), Owen Nolan (1990) and Eric Lindros (1991).*

Facing page, far right: *Québec goalie Ron Tugnutt had a routine night, stopping 21 of 23 shots for his fifth win of the campaign. The remainder of his season was anything but routine as he went winless in 21 decisions (0–18–3).*

GUY LAFLEUR 10

The Flower Ties The Rocket
Vancouver Canucks @ Québec Nordiques – November 11, 1989

For decades, Saturday night in Québec has meant hockey. And the passionate Nordiques fans were certainly treated to an entertaining affair on "ce Samedi soir." In the first period, with the score tied 1–1, a hush went over the crowd when Nordique Paul Gillis tripped Canucks defenceman Paul Reinhart, who was hustling to touch up an icing. Reinhart crashed into the end boards and sprained his ankle, which caused him to miss the next six games. Gillis was not penalized, a fact that left Canucks GM Pat Quinn hot under the collar during his first-intermission radio appearance: "The supervisors [of officials] won't do anything [about referee Ron Hoggarth's missed call] because they're former referees themselves. It's a buddy system."

As it turned out, the Canucks didn't need a power play, because Greg Adams scored right off the ensuing face-off to give them a 2–1 lead. The highlight of the second period came courtesy of Peter Stastny, who electrified the Nordiques faithful, as he often did, with a goal to knot the game at two.

All of this action only served to set the stage for the historic main event. At the 15-minute mark of the third period, Canucks forward Jim Sandlak was whistled off for high-sticking. On the radio broadcast, colour man Tom Larscheid commented on the penalty before turning the mike back over to Jim: *"Yeah, the Canucks should be a little upset by that one. It didn't look like it warranted a penalty, but we're a long ways away and Hoggarth is right there and called it. But I think that the crowd is getting into the game a little bit and affecting his officiat-*

ing somewhat. He didn't call that one when [Canuck] Lidster hauled down Jackson, but now he sends Sandlak to the box. . . . Fogarty shoots, but McLean makes the save, the puck is in front . . . Lafleur . . . scores! Guy Lafleur, goal number 544! Ties Rocket Richard and that gives Québec a 3–2 lead." After another Larscheid comment, Jim continued: *"[Lafleur] is playing very well. I'm amazed that he could come back after being out for four years like that. He was all alone in front, a rebound and easily put it in."*

"The crowd just erupted when he scored," Jim recalls. "All the announcements around the arena were in French, so there was a little speaker mounted above us in the broadcast area to give us a bilingual version of the scoring. I sure didn't need to wait for a translation on that goal!"

Let's close by sending you back to your radio one last time to pick up the the Colisée's actual PA announcement of Lafleur's milestone goal: *"…et son cinq-cent quarante-quatrième dont carriere il on joint ainsi Maurice Richard au huitième meilleur la histoire conter par le numéro dix, Guy Lafleur [. . . Ovation. . .] assisté le numéro vingt-six Peter Stastny et le numéro quarante-trois Bryan Fogarty. . . ."*

"Québec City was the best road stop in the NHL. The city itself is unique. We stayed at the Hilton, in the old walled city. Nearby, just across the street from the Parliament buildings [the National Assembly], was an outdoor rink. Kids would play night hockey under the lights with the snow falling. It was beautiful." — *JR*

"The Colisée was quite a ways from downtown. They built that rink to showcase a young Jean Beliveau. Although the building wasn't outstanding, the crowds were terrific. People would play trumpets and wear silly hats — very lively. Fans knew every player on every team. They knew good hockey and would give credit to the opposing players." — *JR*

"Québec City had the best hot dogs in the NHL by miles, even better than Montreal's. A middle-aged French-Canadian woman ran the stand. She'd take a slice of good-quality whole-wheat bread and toast it with a wiener inside. That was the trick — toasted bread instead of buns. After practice, the players ran to line up for their 'chiens chauds.' Then they boarded the team bus with their two hot dogs — excellent." — *JR*

QUÉBEC

PERIOD 1 2 3 OT

VAN 2
QUE 3   F   57

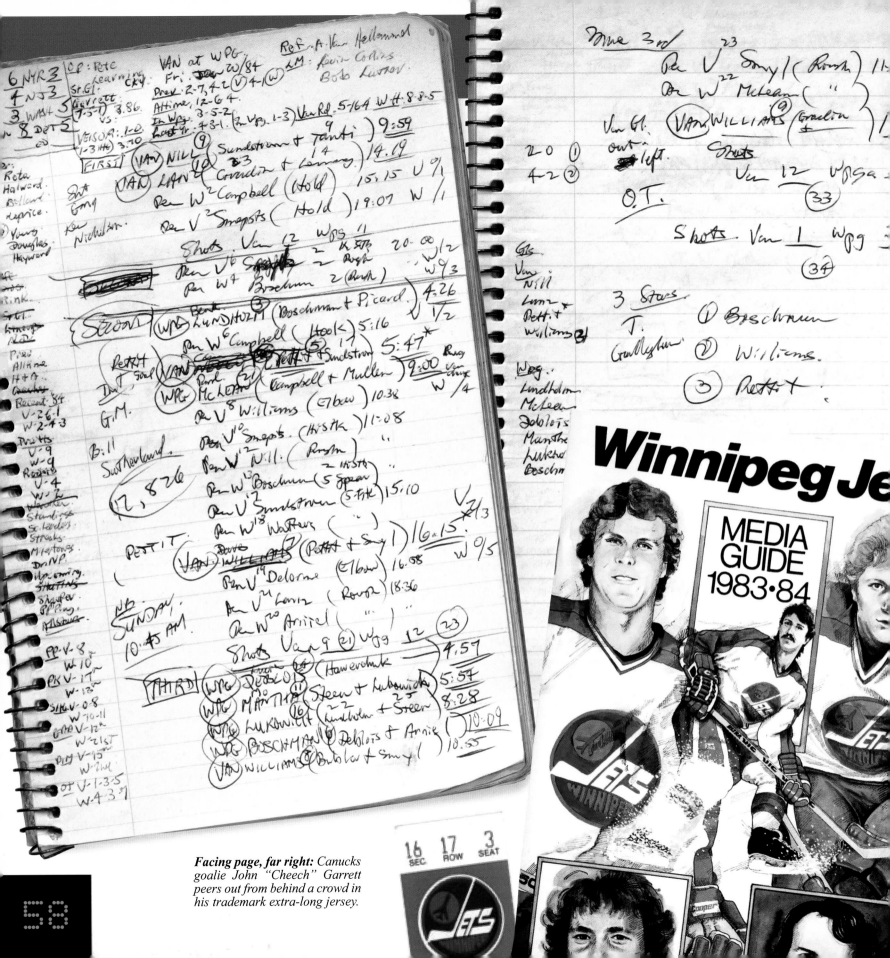

Facing page, far right: Canucks goalie John "Cheech" Garrett peers out from behind a crowd in his trademark extra-long jersey.

(Dr.) Tiger Williams and the Wild West ShoOTout
Vancouver Canucks @ Winnipeg Jets—January 20, 1984

As frequently happened in the 1980s, the Canucks boarded a flight out of Edmonton on the heels of a drubbing by the mighty Oilers. This time they were headed for Winnipeg after absorbing a 7–5 loss, thanks in large part to a routine three-goal, two-assist performance by Gretzky. But this flight was more sombre than most: that loss cost respected Canucks coach Roger Neilson his job. En route to Winnipeg, Canucks goalie John Garrett reflected on the coaching change: "We the players should have recognized months ago that this was going to happen and done something about it to help him. It's too late now… we let him down… it's as simple as that."

Garrett and his mates may have been too late for Neilson, but they responded with a spirited effort against the Winnipeg Jets in support of their GM — and now new coach — Harry Neale. The goaltending matchup pitted two wily veterans: Garrett and the Jets' Mike Veisor, both of whom broke into the big leagues in 1973–74. From there they took different paths. Veisor went to the NHL, but recorded only 59 decisions over seven years as the perennial backup to Tony Esposito in Chicago. Conversely, Garrett was a standout in the WHA, playing in 323 games in six seasons, plus another 52 after his Whalers joined the NHL. In 1980–81, Veisor was dealt to the Whalers and served as their backup until Garrett was traded away the following season. On this night in Winnipeg, the two former teammates met up again; it was perhaps fitting that they backstopped their teams to a tie — the last of Garrett's career. For Veisor, Winnipeg marked the end of the line for his career, despite a respectable 4–1–2 record as a Jet.

The game featured a frenzy of scoring, commonplace in the run-and-gun Smythe Division. At 19:41 of the third period, with the Canucks trailing 6–5 and their goalie pulled, Dave "Tiger" Williams dribbled in a shot against Veisor and the game went into overtime — newly introduced into the NHL that season. The goal completed the Tiger's first-ever NHL hat trick and was greeted by cheers from the otherwise hostile crowd. "The Canucks used to get a lot of reaction in Winnipeg," says Jim, "particularly when they had Tiger Williams, who was a high-profile player. Several hundred fans would drive to Winnipeg from his hometown of Weyburn, Saskatchewan, to cheer for him and the Canucks." Having satisfied his fans, the always quotable Williams satisfied the postgame media as well by musing, "Most of us in this game are general practitioners. Only a few can be brain surgeons. Tonight I performed the operation."

"Winnipeg is a great hockey town. The Winnipeg Arena was great, too. It had a good broadcast booth that hung over the boards, although there was no table for my notes. At one end of the rink was a huge portrait of Queen Elizabeth. The players treated it as a target and shot pucks at it during the pregame warmups." — *JR*

"Winnipeg had a really positive hockey atmosphere, no rivalry. Going in there I was always reminded that hockey really is Canada's game." — *JR*

"Sometimes I got to know the guys who worked in the road press boxes. That was definitely true in Winnipeg, which had a really friendly press box. The broadcast area and the area for reporters were sort of connected. We all used to have meals in there before the game." — *JR*

"In road buildings we had no say over who was our broadcast engineer. But that wasn't the case in Winnipeg, where we got rid of one of the broadcast engineers. He was drinking on the job and I just wasn't comfortable with that." — *JR*

WINNIPEG

PERIOD 1 2 3 OT

VAN 6
WIN 6
F OT

Right: Pre-season tickets to the Sharks first game—ever!

Facing right: Jim's opening-night press pass to the Sharks' first NHL regular-season home game. Jim also called the Sharks' road opener the night before, a 4–3 loss to the Canucks in Vancouver.

Bottom middle: Puck signed by #18, Igor Larionov.

"Crazy George was always a fun part of Bay Area hockey. He was a college teacher who got his cheerleading start in the Oakland Coliseum doing Seals hockey when the crowds were small. Starting in the late 1970s he brought his act to Empire Stadium in Vancouver and pumped up fans of the soccer Whitecaps and the football Lions." — JR

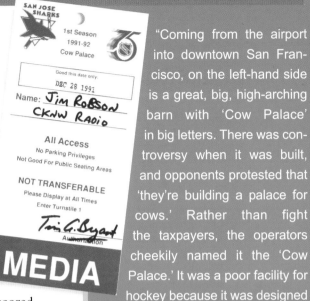

Despite being held pointless in his first 13 games of the season, Canucks' Igor Larionov was starting to round into the form that had made him a star in the Russian Elite league for eight seasons before his escape to North America. As his coach, Pat Quinn, explained: "Igor had a lot of things on his mind with what was going on in the Soviet Union. He was playing like his career was over. Now there's a spark, that mental sharpness which lets you understand how he played so well all those years."

Against the Sharks, Larionov centred an all-European line with Robert Kron and rookie Pavel Bure. Down 1–0 early in the first, Larionov drew the Canucks even with 1:53 showing on the clock. That is, 1:53 gone in the first, not 1:53 remaining. In North American arenas, the timers count down from 20:00 to 0:00 — except, as Jim points out, in San Francisco's old Cow Palace. "There they time the European way. Periods went from 0:00 to 20:00 so you could look at the clock and actually get the right time."

Tough guy Link Gaetz restored the San Jose lead a few minutes later with one of his six career NHL goals — while playing on the power play, no less. Known for his lack of on-ice judgment, the "Missing Link" was true to form, amassing six minutes in roughing penalties as well. But Larionov responded with two more goals to give the Canucks all the offence they would need, as they won 3–2. Larionov's second goal of the night came when the Canucks were short-handed, and his game winner was on the power play. Not only did Igor score all the Canuck goals, he scored them all in the second period and he scored them in all three types of man-power situations: even strength, shorthanded and on the power play.

Such was the skill and versatility that Larionov displayed for a remarkable 14 years in the NHL. His conduct off the ice was equally classy. Jim took note of that early on, and pays Igor one of the highest compliments when he says, "He's a terrific person and a nice man. Igor was Roger Neilson on skates. I wish they could have kept him in Vancouver."

But the Canucks' understandable refusal to pay the Russian Federation any more money after the Vladimir Krutov debacle and lawsuit forced Igor to play in Europe for a season before being placed on waivers by Vancouver. Ironically, having witnessed first-hand Larionov's skill in all facets of the game, San Jose claimed him starting for the 1993–94 season. He went on to win three Stanley Cups with the Detroit Red Wings, and retired in 2004 after 900 games of NHL service.

"Coming from the airport into downtown San Francisco, on the left-hand side is a great, big, high-arching barn with 'Cow Palace' in big letters. There was controversy when it was built, and opponents protested that 'they're building a palace for cows.' Rather than fight the taxpayers, the operators cheekily named it the 'Cow Palace.' It was a poor facility for hockey because it was designed for rodeos and agricultural fairs. The ice wasn't full size and the seats were well back from the ice, with a poor slope. — *JR*

"The first time I was in the Cow Palace was in the minor leagues. I was struck by how much everybody drank. There were bars in every corner of the rink serving hard stuff, not just beer. I think fans took it back to their seats. It was a wild place." — *JR*

"Dennis Hull used to do the colour for the Sharks games for the first few years, and he's a lot of fun. He didn't last very long, I think because he didn't say enough — which is funny, because he's a great speaker on the banquet circuit." — *JR*

SAN JOSE

PERIOD 1 2 3 OT

VAN 3
SJ 2   F   61

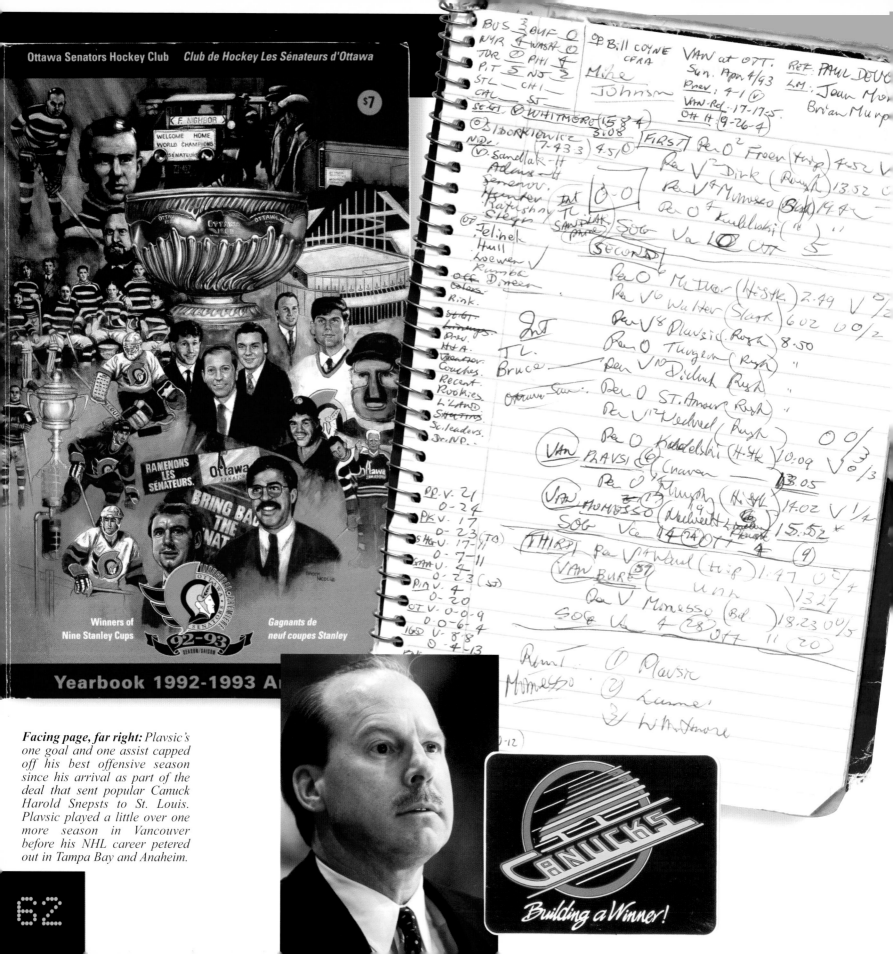

Facing page, far right: Plavsic's one goal and one assist capped off his best offensive season since his arrival as part of the deal that sent popular Canuck Harold Snepsts to St. Louis. Plavsic played a little over one more season in Vancouver before his NHL career petered out in Tampa Bay and Anaheim.

Vancouver Exorcises 70-year-old Demons
Vancouver Canucks @ Ottawa Senators – April 4, 1993

Given its status as Canada's capital city, it stands to reason that a great deal of history has been made in Ottawa. And as the Canucks prepared for their first contest against the expansion Senators, history was in the air. In fact, it was almost 70 years to the day since big-league teams from Vancouver and Ottawa had last played each other. In late March 1923, the Vancouver Maroons of the PCHA had played the original Senators for the Stanley Cup in Vancouver. Back then, Ottawa was a powerhouse squad and had beaten Vancouver for the Cup in 1921 and '22. The rivalry dates even farther back: Vancouver's only Cup win (when the team was known as the Millionaires) came against Ottawa in 1915. All those early Cup matches had been played on the coast, however; this was the first visit to the capital by a Vancouver club.

As it turned out, road wins in Ottawa were not hard to come by. When the first-place Canucks rolled into town, the inept Senators had compiled a miserable 9–64–4 record. Furthermore, Ottawa was fresh from a 7–3 crushing the night before in Hartford, in which the home side scored on each of its first four shots. With that loss, the Sens set the league's all-time record for consecutive road losses at 38 – it was actually 40 away from Ottawa but league officials mercifully didn't count neutral-site losses. Ottawa's road futility streak eventually ended at 41, albeit with a tie, on Long Island the next season.

Peter Sidorkiewicz, who had been the victim of Hartford's first three goals before being mercifully yanked, drew the starting goaltending assignment against the Canucks. Sensing an opportunity to rest their own #1 goalie down the stretch, Vancouver countered with backup Kay Whitmore. Coincidentally, Whitmore and Sidorkiewicz had been teammates in Hartford for the previous four seasons. Perhaps unfortunately for Sidorkiewicz, his play as a Whaler had been better than Whitmore's, and he caught the eye of the Senators' scouts, prompting Ottawa to select him in the expansion draft. For his part, Whitmore found himself traded to a more promising situation in Vancouver. On this night, at opposite ends of the rink — and the standings — Whitmore sported a goals-against average of 3.08 on the season, while Sidorkiewicz's had ballooned to 4.51.

To his credit, Sidorkiewicz held his team even in this game until Canucks blueliner Adrien Plavsic scored with a point shot off of a face-off. The rest of the game played out as expected: Ottawa could muster no offence — and only minimal defence — and Whitmore cruised to his first and only shutout as a Canuck, winning 3–0. Vancouverites could now rest: the 70-year-old Ottawa hockey demons had been exorcised at last.

6 ADRIEN PLAVSIC Defence

"Ottawa is a bilingual town — it was like being in Montreal. Like Montreal, the anthem singer is very distinct. He's an older military man who wears his uniform and white gloves when he sings." — *JR*

"For the Senators' first three and a half years, the old Ottawa Civic Centre was home. The rink was a small facility that backed against Frank Clair Stadium [now the home of the CFL's Renegades], where the Rough Riders played. The underside of the football stands formed the roof of the arena." — *JR*

"When Ottawa joined the league, one of the Canucks' equipment trainers — Vancouver east-ender Ed Georgica — joined the new team. Ed and the other trainers are really hard-working guys. Few people realize what long days they endure. Many nights the team would get into a city around 1:00 a.m. The players and media all went to the hotel, but the trainers had to go to the rink and set up the equipment. They might be done that around 4:00 a.m., and then they would have to be back at 9:00 a.m. for practice. The trainers don't make big money, and the grind of their jobs can put a lot of strain on some guys' families." — *JR*

OTTAWA

PERIOD 1 2 3 OT

VAN	3
OTT	0

F

63

Above and facing right: The cavernous Thunderdome in Tampa.

Above right: Jim's game notes indicate that CKNW sports director John Paul (J.P.) McConnell was colour man on the broadcast. J.P. did the odd game and even a few games of Canucks play-by-play too.

64

While travelling from New Jersey to Tampa, the Canucks went from being iced in to hoping the ice would hold up for 60 minutes. Caught in a northeastern snow storm, the team's flight was cancelled, delaying the team for 24 hours in Parsippany, New Jersey. When they finally arrived in Tampa a few hours before game time, the famous Florida humidity was wreaking havoc with the Thunderdome's ice surface. Captain Trevor Linden said of the conditions, "The ice was awful — it was like skating in quicksand."

But in the NHL the show must go on, especially when a whopping 22,924 fans turn out to watch — still about 5,000 shy of a sellout! The game featured Geoff Courtnall staking the Canucks to a 2–0 lead before the Lightning tied it up in the second period on goals by the skilful Petr Klima and Chris Joseph. Defenceman Dave Babych then netted the eventual winner for the Canucks late in the second period. The teams lethargically went through the motions in the scoreless third, mustering only 12 shots on goal between them.

After the game, Canucks' coach and GM Pat Quinn reflected on the fact that his bigger squad was outhit by Tampa Bay. He uncharacteristically stated, "You always want to trade hits for hits, but it didn't hurt us to be a passive team tonight." The remark prompted a Canucks beat writer to note, prophetically, that while the Canucks' lack of midseason physical play might actually have concerned Quinn, his coaching this

season would instead "be measured by his team's playoff performance." Quinn was right not to push the panic button in February; this season, the Canucks would play hockey well into June.

The 3–2 Canucks win turned out to be Jim's only broadcast from the Thunderdome. In those years, interconference play only took the Canucks to Tampa once a year. The team's 1994–95 visit was cancelled because of the NHL lockout, and there was no television coverage for the Canucks' 1995–96 trip — by which point Jim had stopped doing radio play-by-play and was only working televised games. At the start of the 1996–97 season, the Lightning moved from the converted baseball stadium (now home to the Devil Rays of the American League) to their present home, the St. Petersburg Times Forum (formerly the Ice Palace). Thankfully, ice conditions have been better there.

Whether it was the Lightning's inaugural home, Expo Hall, the Thunderdome or the Ice Palace, Jim noticed one constant in Tampa: "The lack of knowledge and lack of interest by the fans. For people at the games, the concentration was not on hockey — it was a spectacle."

"The Thunderdome in Tampa Bay opened in 1993–94 and had a seating capacity of 28,183. The rink was set in the building at an odd angle. There was all kinds of space around the boards without seats, especially at the ends. There they had games for kids going on — like shooting balls at nets, throwing things through hoops and playing darts. During the game, kids could come down and play all these games. They weren't even watching the hockey game. It was like a circus. It was a very un-hockey-like atmosphere." —*JR*

"I had been to Tampa in the 1970s for an NASL soccer game between the Vancouver Whitecaps and the Tampa Bay Rowdies. I filled in for BCTV's John McKeachie on the soccer broadcast." —*JR*

"Just because Florida is filled with hundreds of thousands of Canadian 'snowbirds' doesn't mean hockey will survive there. Most of them moved to Florida because they don't like hockey." —*JR*

TAMPA BAY

PERIOD 1 2 3 OT

VAN	3	
TB	2	F

Working his Way Up

"*My first pro broadcast was the Edmonton Flyers versus the Vancouver Canucks. It was a Western League game on Grey Cup weekend, 1956. Bill Stephenson was the Vancouver broadcaster, and he'd gone to the Grey Cup in Toronto because he also did football. When he was on another assignment, I would do his job because I was his assistant.*"

In 1968, Jim applied to baseball's Seattle Pilots to be their everyday broadcaster. He'd previously done ten years of Pacific Coast League baseball in Vancouver and used to re-create broadcasts of out-of-town baseball games. According to Jim, the Pilots "didn't want a Canadian broadcaster." The Pilots moved to Milwaukee after one season. "It was a blessing I didn't get that job. Imagine if I had gone. Someone else would have got the NHL job in Vancouver and I would have been out on the street."

Jim received some early attention for his NHL work when the Toronto Telegram *noted, "Jim Robson calling play in last night's NHL All-Star Game [from Madison Square Garden in New York, 1972] was a new voice to us but sounded good enough to keep in mind in case the Hewitt clan ever relaxes its grip on that job." In typical fashion, Jim recalls being "prepared to the hilt for that game."*

PLAY BY PLAY HOCKEY FROM JIM ROBSON, THE GREAT HOCKEY NUT HIMSELF!

CKNW/98
the hockey nut station

Above: *Jim was front and centre in much of CKNW's hockey promotion throughout the 1970s and '80s.*

The Business of Broadcasting

"*In July 1952, right after finishing at Maple Ridge High School, I took a job writing ads for CJAV in Port Alberni. I earned $100 a month ($82 after deductions), and paid my landlady, Mrs. Wilson, $70. Eventually at CJAV I called Alberni Athletics basketball and then Nanaimo Timbermen lacrosse for CHUB.*

"*In September 1956, CKWX Vancouver hired me for $300 a month. I called basketball, baseball, hockey and football. I worked 231 games in 1961 alone. I was hired away from CKWX by CKNW to broadcast the Canucks starting in September 1970. My salary was $15,000 for the first season, including summertime sports. The longest contract I ever had with CKNW was three years, but usually it was just year-to-year.*

"*One season, I didn't think CKNW's first offer was high enough. I mentioned it to Allan McEachern, a high-profile lawyer (later Chief Justice of British Columbia) who I got to know in his capacity as president of the BC Lions. All he said was, 'Leave it to me.' He arranged a luncheon at the old University Club, just west of Burrard on Hastings, for Allan, [CKNW manager] Mel Cooper and myself. We had a nice lunch, but no discussion of contract or anything. I was wondering what was going on, and at the end of the lunch, Allan said, 'Mel, that offer to Jim isn't good enough. You can do better than that.' That's all he said, and we all said our goodbyes. And sure enough, CKNW did do better. Allan never sent me a bill, he just did that as a friend. I was never comfortable with the negotiating side of the business.*

"*CKNW wanted me to do all the games, so when I missed a CKNW game to do Hockey Night in Canada I had to pay my replacement. In the 1970s I used to have to write a cheque to Jim Cox!*

"*Ralph Mellanby, who ran the show at HNiC, was in my corner. We talked about me moving to Toronto, but it never worked out. HNiC was not easy to deal with. They'd send you an agreement with the price and say 'Take it or leave it.' There wasn't much negotiation.*"

Relationship with the Players

"I did my work and I didn't socialize with the players. The coach who influenced me most in the early years was Bert Olmstead. The guys were afraid of him because he was a tough coach and a tough player. But Bert was always fine with me and he really knew hockey. When I rode on the team bus in the mid-sixties, he'd say to me, 'You're riding on our bus. What happens on this bus stays on this bus. You're a guest on this bus.' I would be on the bus early because they weren't going to hold the bus up for me. I'd always sit in my same seat and let the players get off the bus first. When my career was winding down, the older players would hold up and say to me, 'Nope, we're not leaving until you get off the bus.' That was a nice gesture.

"I prided myself on not hanging out with the players. But you could quite often tell, the next morning on the bus, which ones might have stayed out too long or had too much to drink. Rarely did I go along with the players on social excursions while we were on the road. However, I did once with the Western League Canucks down in San Diego. We had some real characters on that team, including Hank Cahan, Don Cherry and Phil Maloney. Maloney in particular was a key guy on the team, and a real practical joker. I tagged along on a day off when the guys all went down to Tijuana, Mexico. Cherry went into a shop and bought a huge ceramic vase for his wife, Rose. Seeing this, Maloney went into the shop after Cherry had left and bought an identical vase. Later that evening, we were all sitting around the pool [back at the hotel] at about nine in the evening, and the guys were drinking and swimming and acting up a bit. Maloney came out on Cherry's second-floor balcony overlooking the pool — holding the duplicate vase — and called down, 'Hey Grapes, is this the vase you bought for Rose?' At which point he fumbled and dropped it. The vase fell and smashed on the concrete below. Grapes was fuming until he found out it was all a big joke."

Right: Jim fields hockey questions from students at the Pacific National Exhibition (PNE), just one of his countless public appearances over the years.

The Listening Audience

"Canucks radio broadcasts had the biggest audience of anywhere in the NHL. The Canucks were listened to by more people than in New York, Boston and Toronto. In all those cities there is so much more TV, so the radio was never as prominent. Also, in Montreal there's the English/French split, so there is no dominant broadcast.

"I was aware that the audience was mostly Vancouver and British Columbia, and they were Canucks fans. So when the Canucks scored I was more excited than when the other team scored. But I didn't colour that by covering up mistakes or taking away from an opponent's play. I think people in Canada want an honest job — I don't think they want a 'homer' job. But I think now that has changed. I think it has become showbiz and some guys are just cheerleading. That American influence is there."

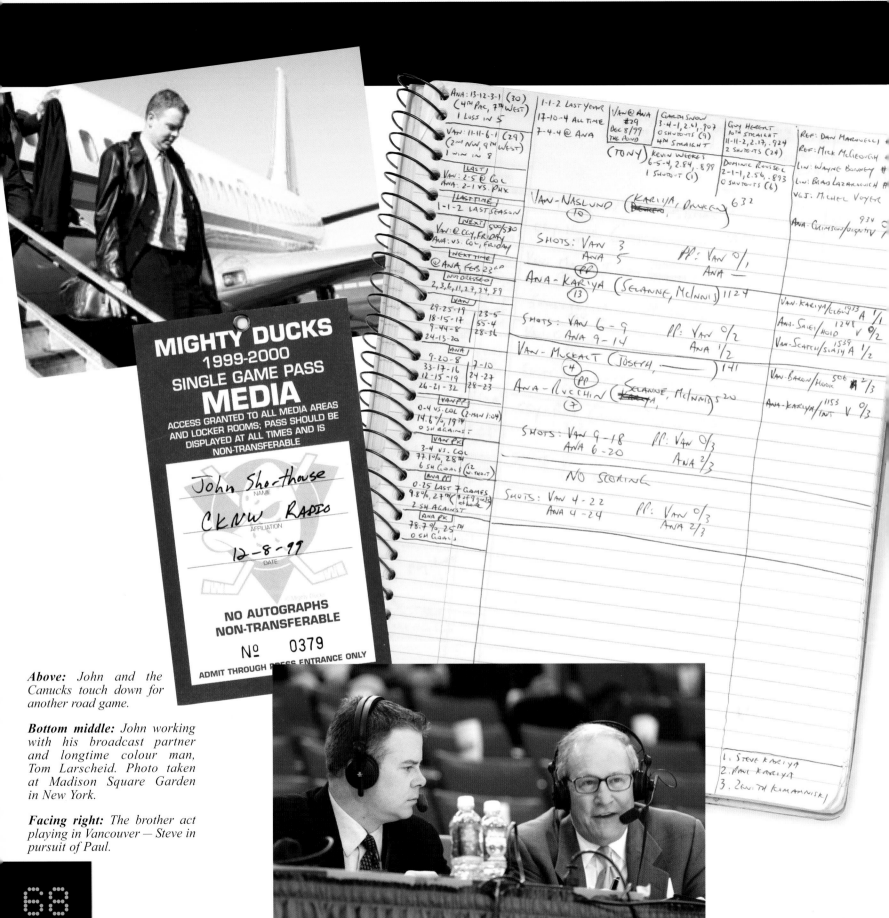

Above: John and the Canucks touch down for another road game.

Bottom middle: John working with his broadcast partner and longtime colour man, Tom Larscheid. Photo taken at Madison Square Garden in New York.

Facing right: The brother act playing in Vancouver — Steve in pursuit of Paul.

MIGHTY DUCKS
1999-2000
SINGLE GAME PASS
MEDIA
ACCESS GRANTED TO ALL MEDIA AREAS AND LOCKER ROOMS; PASS SHOULD BE DISPLAYED AT ALL TIMES AND IS NON-TRANSFERABLE

John Shorthouse
NAME

CKNW RADIO
AFFILIATION

12-8-99
DATE

NO AUTOGRAPHS
NON-TRANSFERABLE

№ 0379
ADMIT THROUGH PRESS ENTRANCE ONLY

Oh Brother, Don't Make Me 'Kiss My Sister'
Vancouver Canucks @ Anaheim Mighty Ducks–December 8, 1999

I t's been said that a tie hockey game is akin to "kissing your sister." In the low-scoring NHL of the late 1990s, sisters everywhere were saying "enough!" The Canucks and the Mighty Ducks of Anaheim were no strangers to ties, having sawed off both their previous meetings at Arrowhead Pond.

There was also a fraternal connection in this game: For the first time, Ducks superstar Paul Kariya lined up against his younger brother, Steve, a rookie forward striving to keep a job with the Canucks. Because of a three-year age difference, the brothers had never played competitive hockey against each other. Sensing a rare opportunity, Canucks coach Marc Crawford put Steve on the ice for the opening face-off.

We send you to the Pond in Anaheim, just moments away from the drop of the puck. Here's your broadcast team of Tom Larscheid (TL) and John Shorthouse (JS):

TL: *"Well, the Kariya brothers are right next to each other. I'm just looking to see if they're talking. Doesn't look like they are. They're ready to compete."*

JS: *"And off the draw they separate after Steve put the stick in the midsection of Paul for an instant—and away we go! Cassels, Naslund and Steve Kariya out for Vancouver to start the game as Steve puts the puck into the zone deep. Canucks go in on the forecheck . . ."*

So began 65 minutes of even, tight-checking hockey that produced a final

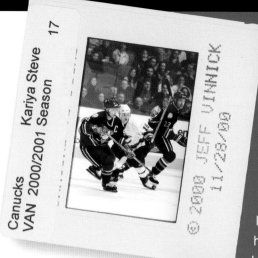

shot count of only 24–22 in favour of the home team. The brothers, however, distinguished themselves despite the lack of free-wheeling play that better suits their skills. Steve started things off with an assist on the game's first goal, while big brother Paul countered with the Ducks' first goal, midway through the second period. Paul's goal came on the power play — with none other than Steve in the box, serving an elbowing penalty. Not to be outdone, and with the score tied 2–2 in the third period, mild-mannered Paul took a rare penalty for interference, but the Ducks killed it off — along with any hopes the Canucks might leave Anaheim with two points.

The brothers were named the first two stars of the game. Thereafter, Paul's career continued to flourish, while Steve battled the stigma of being too small to play in the NHL. "I think he would have had a shot in a different era," says John. "He hit the NHL at the exact wrong time — the obstruction, the trap and everything just worked against him. You look at some of the games he played in that season [1999–2000], and he really did find some chemistry with Alex Mogilny. Steve is kind of Cliff Ronning-ish, but in a different time."

"Arrowhead Pond is one of the newfangled 'cookie-cutter' rinks. [Colour man] Tom Larscheid and I are a long way from the action. Tom's brother often sits in the smallish booth with us, as he lives nearby and is a huge Canucks fan via the Internet." — *JS*

"Our Anaheim and L.A. operator is Tony Noto. Tony is a real character and he loves to kibitz, and he'll even pop up on the air sometimes for fun. He has a large nose that Larscheid thinks looks like Jimmy Durante — all those references kind of fly over my head. They are forever doing Jimmy Durante imitations. The Durante influence also cropped up one night in Anaheim after Ed Jovanovski scored in overtime. Tom's spontaneous and jubilant one-liner was, 'Good night Mrs. Calabash, wherever you are!'" — *JS*

"Hockey knowledge in Anaheim is pretty good now — they don't announce offside calls in the building anymore. [Former NHL goalie] Brian Hayward works on Ducks broadcasts and is regarded as one of the better colour analysts and teachers of the game." — *JS*

ANAHEIM

* * * *

PERIOD 1 2 3 OT

VAN	**2**	**F OT**
ANA	**2**	

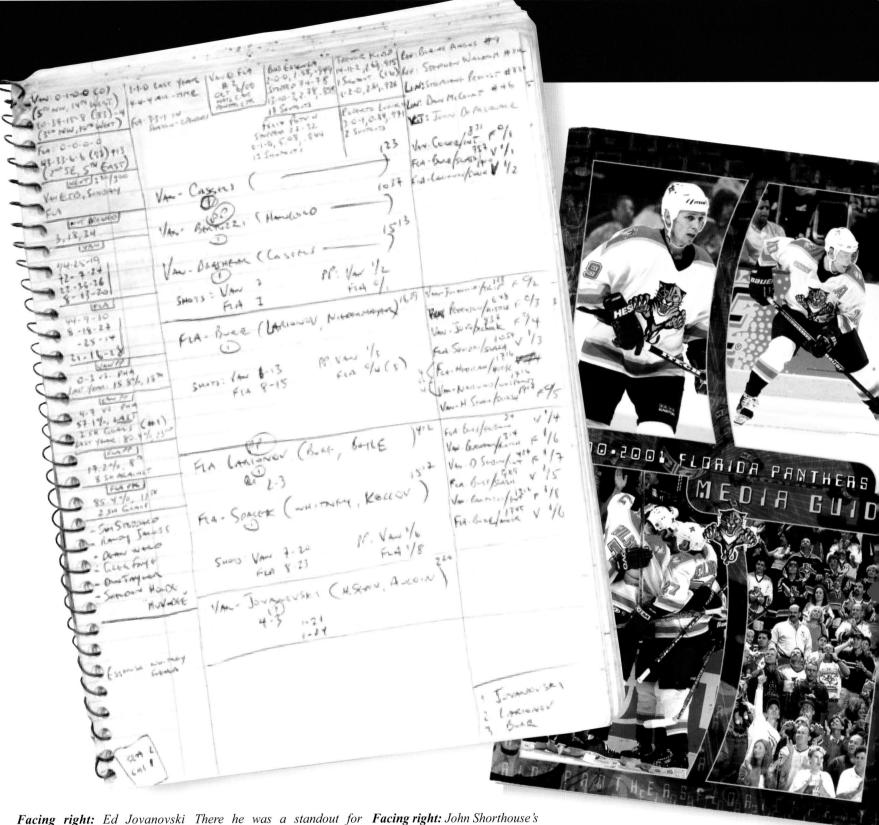

Facing right: Ed Jovanovski was drafted 1st overall in the 1994 Entry Draft by Florida. There he was a standout for three and a half years before being traded to Vancouver in a blockbuster deal that gave Pavel Bure his desired fresh start in Florida. *Facing right: John Shorthouse's press pass from an earlier visit to Miami.*

All the talk heading into the Panthers' season opener centred on the match-up between Florida's Pavel Bure and the Canucks' Ed Jovanovski, who had been traded for one another in January 1999. Bure's exit from Vancouver had been acrimonious, having been brought about by a contract holdout, followed by a return to Russia. But now the time had come to face his old team.

Both players did what they do best: Defenceman Jovanovski registered five hits in the first period alone, while Bure lit the lamp once and set up another. The Bure goal was the first of three for the Panthers, which erased a 3–0 Canucks lead and sent the game into overtime, when Jovanovski stole the show by scoring the game-winner on a backhand deke.

"There was a great reaction from the fans in the stands [in Florida], who were big Ed Jovanovski fans," John recalls. "They date back to the clashes Jovo had with the Flyers' Eric Lindros during Florida's Cinderella playoff run to the finals in 1996. Florida fans certainly had fond memories of Ed Jovanovski." However, when asked if he remembers the overtime goal itself, John candidly replies, "No, not really. That game was at an early stage of my career, and if an OT goal got scored I just kinda lost my mind. I probably blew a few brain cells making the call. I should listen to it sometime." Okay, how about now? Here's a replay of Jovo's OT winner against Bure and the Panthers:

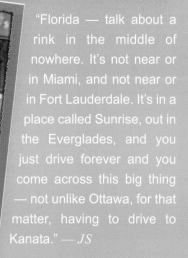

"Aucoin steals a pass at centre. Here's Henrik [Sedin] over the Florida line, in front for [twin brother] Daniel. It comes to Jovanovski, in on goal . . . scores!! . . . Ed Jovanovski against his old team has won it in overtime!! . . . There's your final: Canucks 4, Florida 3."

Shorty's Stories:

"Once when the team was in Florida, [Canucks captain Mark] Messier arranged to have his yacht and crew come up to take the hockey team out cruising — a team bonding exercise. When I arrived in town, I remember being summoned. Some underling player came to my seat at the front of the team bus and said 'Mark would like to talk to you.' So I made the walk to the back of the bus, wondering what I'd said about him on the air that he didn't appreciate. To my surprise, he invited me on the cruise — which was really cool, except that I couldn't go as I had work to do for a deadline. But Mark was good that way — on a couple of occasions, I've been in a restaurant that Mark was at, and I've found out that my meal had been bought or there was a bottle of wine coming."— JS

"Florida — talk about a rink in the middle of nowhere. It's not near or in Miami, and not near or in Fort Lauderdale. It's in a place called Sunrise, out in the Everglades, and you just drive forever and you come across this big thing — not unlike Ottawa, for that matter, having to drive to Kanata." — JS

"One thing American fans are into is the gear and paraphernalia. There might only be 7,000 people in the seats, but 6,000 of them are wearing a jersey — a completely different sight from a Canadian rink." — JS

"Ice conditions are always a factor in Florida because of the humidity. The league has made a concerted effort in the last few years to get a uniform ice standard and then improve it, and they've done a good job. It's probably because of the advent of rinks like Florida and Tampa that, after every game, the trainers fill out a report based on what the players tell them about the ice. Then each rink's ice gets rated and they try to fix the ones that aren't as good." — JS

FLORIDA PANTHERS
2000
National Car Rental Center
VISITING TEAM
TV/RADIO
GAME 5
5
vs. Vancouver Canucks
October 20, 1999
NHL
2000

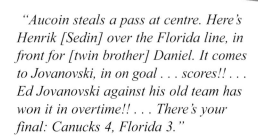

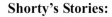

FLORIDA

Above: *Jim and John's game notes from Nashville are fun to compare. Jim called the game for television station VTV and John did the radio broadcast for CKNW.*

NASHVILLE PREDATORS
1998-99 INAUGURAL SEASON

A Grand Ole Firing
Vancouver Canucks @ Nashville Predators – January 19, 1999

Two games after making what was arguably the biggest trade in Canucks history by shipping holdout superstar Pavel Bure to Florida, GM Brian Burke terminated the head coach he'd inherited, Mike Keenan. This whirlwind of events occurred during John Shorthouse's rookie season as the team's radio voice.

Vancouver won its first game after the deal, against the first-place Stars in Dallas. John recalls that one of the newcomers, Dave Gagner, "looked all-world playing with Markus Naslund. Everyone around the team was thinking this is a pretty good deal. All of a sudden Brian Burke looked like a genius. But then the Canucks go into Nashville and lose 4–1 to the first-year Predators," John says. "I didn't think much of it at the time, but it turned out it to be Keenan's last game."

With the All-Star break coming right after the Nashville game, John recalls that Keenan had "organized an impromptu mini-training camp back in Vancouver for everyone except captain Mark Messier whom he excused. Naturally there was some grumbling with the guys about having to practise during the break. Anyhow, I went to San Francisco on a holiday, and the next thing I heard was that Keenan got fired." Burke's comments after the firing seemed to indicate that, in his opinion, Mike Keenan had quit coaching behind the bench.

John's observations on Iron Mike Keenan:

"Mike Keenan is an interesting cat, there's no question. For sure he's hot and cold, and you don't know what you're getting a lot of the time. A lot of his antics he does on purpose, I think. He reveres Scotty Bowman, and Scotty's whole thing was to keep people guessing. Same with Mike — walk in after an 8–0 win and find him sour, walk in after an 8–0 loss and he'd be bouncing off the walls, all giddy." — JS

"Mike wasn't afraid to resort to unorthodox tactics to get his message across — be it to his players or his boss. In a cheeky plea for scoring help, I remember him pulling his goalie in a one-goal game at Toronto with about 15 minutes to go. There was never a dull moment with Keenan behind the bench." — JS

"There was a side of Keenan that most people never see, the happy-go-lucky side. I remember in Philadelphia once . . . we were standing outside the hotel and I said to him, 'Boy, you must have loved living here [when he coached the Flyers].' Rather than answer my question he launched into singing a song about Philadelphia called 'South Street.' He started singing and then just walked away." — JS

TV CREW

Name: JOHN SHORTHOUSE

Affiliation: CKNW

NASHVILLE PREDATORS

G.N.

Good on above date only

"Nashville, home of the Grand Ole Opry, is a neat town but it's not a traditional hockey town. The rink is in a great area for sightseeing and you can hear live music there any time of the day. The hockey club does a good job of bringing the music of the streets into the rink. During warmup and intermissions, a live band plays right behind one of the nets. Also, because of the recording talent in town, Nashville usually gets the best anthem singers." — JS

"For a change, The Gaylord Entertainment Center is not a cookie-cutter rink. Instead it's got an interesting architecture to it, although some of it is weird. The inside uses a purple and yellow motif." — JS

"Our broadcast location is strange. We're at the back of the stands towards the corner of the rink and we don't really have a press box. I usually *stand* in Nashville because they only give us these really uncomfortable metal stools which are too high for the desk so my knees hit the desk when I sit." — JS

NASHVILLE

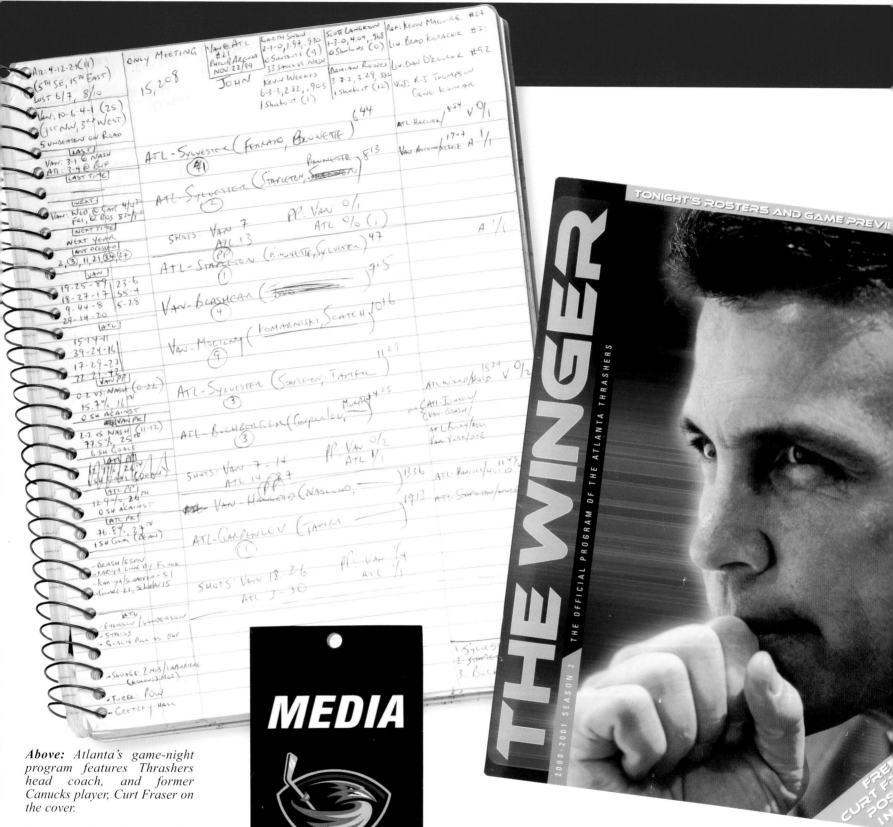

Above: Atlanta's game-night program features Thrashers head coach, and former Canucks player, Curt Fraser on the cover.

Facing right: Thrashers forward Dean Sylvester.

MEDIA

ATLANTA THRASHERS

John Shorthouse
Vancouver TV

THE WINGER

TONIGHT'S ROSTERS AND GAME PREVIEW

THE OFFICIAL PROGRAM OF THE ATLANTA THRASHERS

2000-2001 SEASON 2

Walking to Atlanta's new rink prior to this game gave John a strange feeling. The reason: His path took him through the adjoining Olympic Plaza. "It felt eerie there because my only memory of the Olympic Plaza was the bomb going off during the Summer Games [in 1996]." But heading into the match with the expansion Thrashers, he and the visiting Canucks had the grounds for another unsettling sensation. "The Canucks were off to a good start that year, four games above .500, first in the division and challenging atop the Western Conference," he says. "Then they go into Atlanta against a team that had won only four games all year. It almost felt like it should be a shoo-in . . . but those are the scary ones!"

The Canucks can be forgiven if they weren't familiar with the level of competition the host team might be expected to provide. Vancouver had not yet clashed with the expansion Thrashers; in fact, this marked the first visit to Atlanta by a Canucks team in almost 20 years. They had last played in the Georgia capital on March 10, 1980, when they beat the Flames, 5–2. On that night a rugged sophomore patrolled the left wing for the Canucks on a line with Thomas Gradin and Stan Smyl. The winger's name: Curt Fraser. And although Fraser didn't make a mark on the score sheet that night, he picked up a bit more pro hockey experience — which he was now drawing on as the Thrashers' first-ever bench boss.

The game itself was anything but a classic, and the unlikeliest player emerged as the game's first star. In only his fourth NHL game, Dean Sylvester scored his first three big-league goals, at the same time recording the first hat trick in the Thrashers' short history. "I never thought I'd get three goals and an assist in the same game," said Sylvester after his scoring outburst. "It's a dream to play in the NHL, and to get a hat trick is that much better." Sylvester's dream ended after 92 more games, in which he counted 18 more goals.

"The Philips Center is an interesting design; all of their box seating is on one side. There's a big bank of luxury boxes stacked on top of each other and it forms a big wall; and above that there are seats going up the rest of the way. It's certainly not like most rinks that have two rings of luxury boxes in the middle. Fans wanting to do the wave in Atlanta would definitely suffer." — *JS*

"The Thrashers hired Scotty Ferrall in their first year to be the radio broadcaster. He was big on MTV Sports, but the guy was a complete nut bar. When Atlanta scored, he'd say something like 'I need a freshie! I need a freshie! [meaning a fresh beer].' During broadcasts he had a mike mounted on the end of a hockey stick, and he'd stand in the booth and scream into it. Whenever I'd glance over he looked like a crazy wild man who was going to cross-check someone. He only lasted a year. I guess the Thrashers were just trying to make a splash in the new market." — *JS*

ATLANTA

PERIOD 1 2 3 OT

VAN 3
ATL 6   F

75

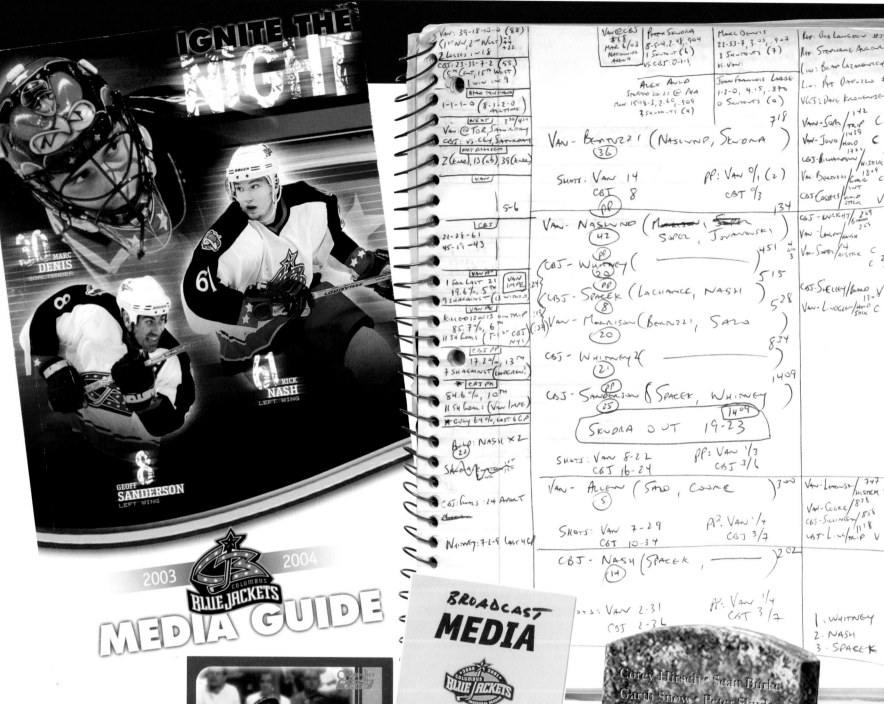

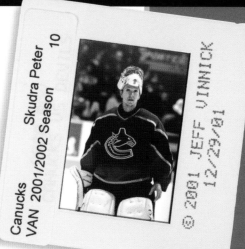

Skudra Peter 10
Canucks VAN 2001/2002 Season
© 2001 JEFF VINNICK 12/29/01

Much has been made about the site of the Columbus Blue Jackets' rink, the Nationwide Arena, which is built on what was once the site of the Ohio State Penitentiary. On Easter Sunday of 1930, 322 inmates perished in a fire that swept through the prison while the guards, fearing a mass escape, kept the facility locked down. That fire remains the single worst disaster in the history of the U.S. penal system. Legend has it that the grounds are haunted to this day by those who perished in the fire.

And while stories of ghosts and goblins may be a hot topic of pregame conversation among visiting players, Canucks starting goalie Peter Skudra was trying to overcome being spooked by another source of ghosts: Vancouver's notorious hockey goalie graveyard. Consider that in the six seasons since long-time #1 goalie Kirk McLean was traded away, a whopping total of 18 other men have seen action defending the Vancouver goal. Skudra surely entered the game feeling as if his burial plot was being readied. As John recalls, "Clearly he was losing the confidence of his coach [Marc Crawford]." Skudra had been pulled in Philadelphia the game before, after giving up a pair of goals on the only three shots he faced. Despite his solid 18–13–6 record since coming to Vancouver, and his 2.48 goals-against average on the season, Skudra had become the victim of soft goals. As John puts it, "He started letting in those deflating goals that can kill a team" —

and that prove fatal to one's job in pro hockey.

Against the Blue Jackets, who were in the Western Conference basement at the time, Skudra again faltered. Crawford pulled him at 14:09 of the second period after the netminder allowed his fourth goal in a 9:18 stretch that erased a 2–0 Canucks lead and left them playing catch-up on the road. The Canucks did score in the third period to send the game into overtime, but an emerging young gun, Rick Nash, scored on a breakaway against backup goalie Alex Auld to win it for Columbus.

"Even then you could see how good Rick Nash was going to be," John remembers. "Nash was still a teenager and had hardly started to fill out, but he was a real big boy. He also had great talent with that Bertuzzi-like combination of skill and brawn. From my standpoint, it's fun to see guys like that at such an early stage in their career. It's like a colt — you're waiting for him to mature into the racehorse, you can see all the potential." And so while Nash was unfazed by any penitentiary ghosts, the spectres managed to haunt Peter Skudra who, only three appearances later, was consigned to Vancouver's goalie graveyard.

"Attached to Nationwide Arena is a really cool practice facility. That's the dream of any NHL trainer, to have both facilities right there so he doesn't have to lug equipment around. For instance, I know the trek in Vancouver from GM Place to Burnaby Eight Rinks is a real hassle. But back to Columbus. In front of the main rink they also built a big brick plaza with a huge outdoor TV screen. Fans that don't have a ticket to the game can sit in the plaza, have a meal and a beer, and watch the game on the TV. During games it becomes a bit of a party atmosphere there. Each year when we go back there's more and more stuff popping up near the rink. The whole area is starting to become urban chic." — *JS*

"Not much else notable in Columbus except that we have a cool flat-screen monitor there and our engineer's name is Scoop — which I think is a good name." — *JS*

COLUMBUS

PERIOD 1 2 3 OT

VAN 4
CBJ 5 **F OT**

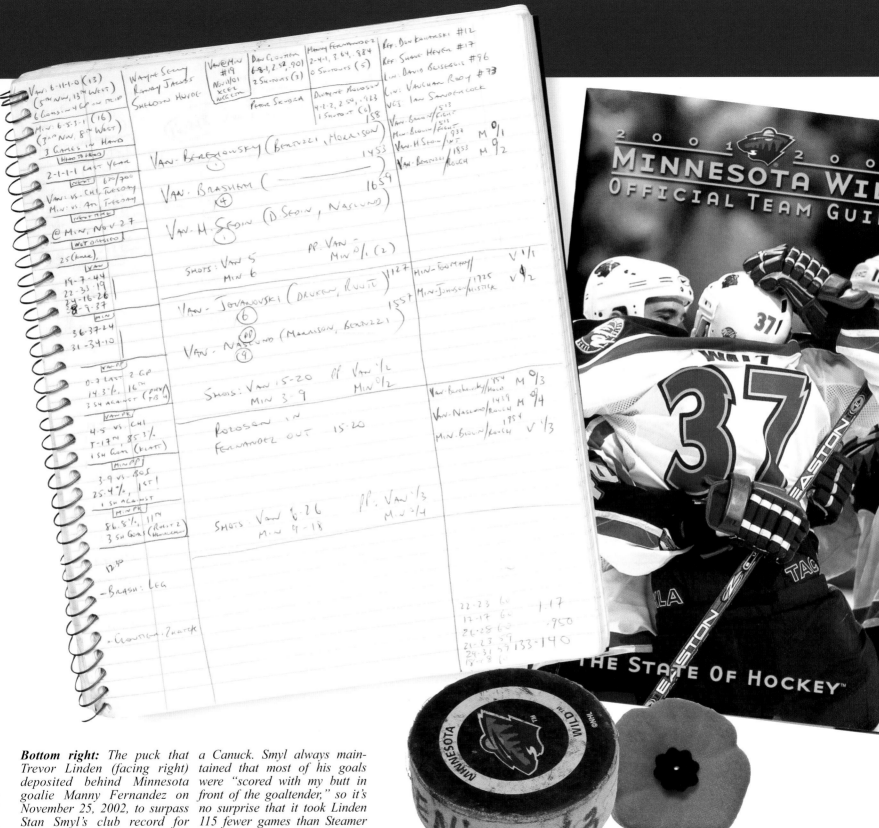

Bottom right: *The puck that Trevor Linden (facing right) deposited behind Minnesota goalie Manny Fernandez on November 25, 2002, to surpass Stan Smyl's club record for career regular-season goals by a Canuck. Smyl always maintained that most of his goals were "scored with my butt in front of the goaltender," so it's no surprise that it took Linden 115 fewer games than Steamer to set the record.*

Some people mark special occasions with a bottle of champagne. Others may record memorable events on film. Not Trevor Linden: He just travels to Minnesota. At least that's what he did when he scored his first NHL hat trick in 1988 (see pages 24–25). He would also find his way to Minnesota in November 2002 to score his 263rd regular-season goal as a Canuck, overtaking Stan Smyl for the franchise record. So it was only fitting that, when he was reacquired after an absence of almost four years, the first item on his "to do" list was to meet the team for a game in Minnesota.

For Linden, the trade from Washington back to Vancouver — the site of his greatest team and personal accomplishments — was emotional. "To be able to come home and play at home again — that's what I call it — and to be part of an organization that has meant a lot to me, is special," said Linden after the Minnesota game. But as John Shorthouse points out, "There weren't many Canucks players that remembered him from before — Markus Naslund, Mattias Ohlund, and that might have been it. Trevor's return certainly wasn't like a reunion for the other players. But the rest of us [media and team staff] all understood the significance of his return."

Linden was (re)joining a youthful team trying to get to the next level — and in need of an extra veteran with deep playoff experience to do so.

Wearing his familiar Canucks jersey #16 — now adorned with an A to signify his status as alternate captain — Linden played a solid game. He centred Matt Cooke and Trent Klatt and the Canucks won handily 5–0 over the second-year Wild team. John points out that Canucks centre Andrew Cassels was injured at the time, and so "Linden played quite a bit and had an unbelievable night in the face-off circle."

In what would become a more competitive and heated rivalry in years to come, the Canucks outplayed the Wild, outshot them 26–18, and received much steadier goaltending in posting the shutout victory. That win was the start of a four-game unbeaten streak and the Canucks eventually rose from five games below .500 to finish the season 12 games over. Linden's presence during that resurgence was no coincidence.

"The Xcel Energy Center is a neat rink, coloured in a really nice forest green. It is the only rink in the league where you can get fried walleye — a freshwater fish." — *JS*

"Minnesota has great hockey tradition and passionate, knowledgeable fans. It's just sad that since their reincarnation they have had such a boring team to watch. In the past, Minnesota's grassroots hockey culture actually hurt the professional teams. When the North Stars died, it was as if people preferred going to high-school games. What a turnaround — since the team came back as the Wild, I don't believe there has ever been an unsold ticket in Minnesota." — *JS*

"Before every game the Minnesota fans do some sort of chant. I'm not sure if it turns into a song at some point, but between the anthem and the opening face-off everyone in the rink chants, 'Let's play hockey!' For each game, they pick someone different to lead the chant, but it's always someone from the past. They choose people like Neal Broten or other guys with ties to Minnesota hockey." — *JS*

MINNESOTA

PERIOD 1 2 3 OT

VAN 5
MIN 0
F

Wild: Gretzky Takes John Garrett's Car... in Four Parts

35th NHL All-Star Game, Uniondale, New York

Campbell Conference 9 @ Wales Conference 3 — February 8, 1983

Canucks backup goalie John Garrett sparkled in net as a substitute for his injured All-Star teammate, Richard Brodeur. As Jim tells it: "Garrett came in in the middle of the second period and made about seven or eight great saves. By the end of the period, all the media were talking about Garrett [having a chance at] winning the car awarded to the All-Star Game's most valuable player." But partway into the third, Wayne Gretzky scored for Garrett's Campbell squad. "After the goal," Jim carries on, "I saw Lanny McDonald of the Campbells skate back to Garrett and say something, and I could see them having a laugh. A few minutes later, Gretzky scored again

against Wales goalie Pelle Lindbergh, and again McDonald skated back and said something to Garrett and they chuckled. "This routine happened two more times as Gretzky scored an All-Star–record four goals in the period. After the game, Garrett told me that McDonald came back after the first goal and said something like, 'They might give the seats in your car to Gretz.' Then 'Your car might not have a steering wheel' after the second goal; 'He's got your engine' after the third goal; and finally, 'Your car belongs to Wayne.'" Garrett may not have won the car, but he did post a win in his only NHL All-Star Game appearance.

Jim broadcast the game for Canadian TV, while his longtime friend Dan Kelly handled the U.S. chores. Jim remembers getting together with Dan after the game, but that "Dan was steaming because he called the wrong guy on the first goal. It's easy to do at an All-Star Game because some of the players don't wear their regular number. Nevertheless, he was still so mad at himself. That's the way play-by-play guys are. Riding home on the bus, you think, 'What did I do wrong? What did I leave out?' You run through it all over and over. Some nights it goes okay, but you never have a perfect game."

For the 1983 match, the CBC decided that its broadcasters would wear tuxedos. Jim recalls having to pin up his pants with a safety pin at the hotel because they kept on sagging. At the rink, Jim was doing a 45-second on-camera opening for HNiC when

a voice in his earpiece said, "There's a delay. You have to fill." The agony of that moment comes flooding back to Jim today as he recounts what happened next: "My face probably went all red and I just babbled along, waiting for someone to get me out of it. To make matters worse, my safety pin popped open while I was babbling and my rental pants dipped, so I was very uncomfortable."

Weird: Flyers 'in a Fog' Against the Sabres

Philadelphia Flyers 2 @ Buffalo Sabres 4 – May 22, 1975

Fresh off an overtime win in game three of the 1975 Cup Finals, the Sabres looked to use every possible home-ice advantage to win game four and tie the series. Although fog wasn't in their plans, it seemed to foil the Flyers. The May heat combined with the crowd and the Buffalo Auditorium's lack of air-conditioning meant patches of fog formed at ice-level. Jim recalls the scene being "not too bad from a broadcast standpoint, but the visibility for the goalies was definitely compromised. During stoppages in play, the gates behind the net to my right would open up and a half dozen kids would skate out waving towels on the end of sticks to break up the fog. Even some of the players lent a helping hand to clear it up."

Earlier in the series, called by Jim on Hockey Night in Canada, there was another weird incident. Just as the players were getting ready to face off, a bat came down from the rafters and started flying around near the ice. Jim Lorentz of the Sabres swung his stick at it and knocked it out of the air. During the play-by-play I said something like, 'There's a bird in the way and Lorentz has knocked it out of the air with his stick and killed it." Well, it wasn't a bird it was a bat, but I didn't know that. Apparently CBC started getting calls from people who were upset about the nice little bird that was killed. That's when HNiC producer Ralph Mellanby said over the headset, 'For God's sake, tell the people it was a bat not a bird.' From that day on, Lorenz, now the television colour man for the Sabres, has been known as Batman."

Wacky: Tiger Rides His Stick at MLG

Vancouver Canucks 8 @ Toronto Maple Leafs 5 — December 10, 1980

In Tiger Williams' first game at Maple Leaf Gardens after being traded to Vancouver 10 months earlier, he promised $100 to whoever scored the winning goal against his old team. It looked as though he might collect his own prize when he scored midway through the third to put the Canucks up 5–4. "The crowd went wild when Tiger scored," says Jim, "because he was so popular and prominent in Toronto." In Tiger's excitement at having scored, he proceeded to ride his stick like a hobby horse the length of the ice. According to Jim, "The Toronto fans enjoyed his celebratory antics even more." But it was Williams' linemate Per-Olov Brasar who had the last laugh on this night. Brasar scored the Canucks' sixth goal in the 8–5 win over the Leafs, and in doing so collected Tiger's $100 award.

PERIOD 1 2 3 OT INTERMISSION

Above: Jim Robson broadcasting a charity game with Jim Hughson. Hughson carried on the high standards of Canucks game broadcasts whenever Robson had Hockey Night in Canada *commitments, and after he first retired.*

Right: Travel by charter plane has been a big improvement over the "no-frills" commercial flights that Jim and the team used to endure, but late-night arrivals and departures are still the norm.

Schedule of Memorable Nights

OCTOBER

		1	2	3	4	5
PIT/FLA 6 '76 / '00	7	8	DET 9 1995	BOS 10 1973	TOR 11 1970	12
13	EDM 14 1979	15	16	17	18	19
20	21	22	23	24	25	26
TOR 27 1971	28	29		PHO 31 2003		

NOVEMBER

					1	2
3	4	5	6	7	EDM 8 1985	9
10	QUE/MIN 11 '89 / '01	12		NJ 14 1996		16
MIN 17 1988	18	19	20		DAL/ATL '95 / '99	23
STL 24 1990	NYR 25 1997		CAR 27 2002		29	30

 HOME year   AWAY year

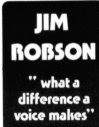

JIM ROBSON

" what a difference a voice makes"

---

overti

ING

a starts 5 minutes and

cue # 24

ductory remarks to:-

CUE # 25:   "I'LL HAVE MORE ON TONIGHT'S

                 MINUTE..."

35 SEC: COMMERCIAL & CREDIT - CLIEN

30 SEC: COMMERCIAL - CLIENT

                 CONTINUATION OF REMARKS TO:-

CUE # 26:   "SOME FINAL COMMENT ON THE G

30 SEC: COMMERCIAL - CLIENT

                 COMMERCIAL & CLIENT

...this is Jim Robson/Al
Good afternoon/Good Night

CART #

CART #

CEMBER

	2	3	4	5	6	7
NA 99	9	**TOR** 10 1980	11	12	13	14
5	16	17	18	19	20	21
2	23	24	25	26	27	**SJ** 28 1991
HIL 72	30	31				

NUARY

		BOS 1 1973	2	3	**COL** 4 1980	
5	6	**MTL** 7 1987	8	9	10	11
12	13	14	15	**PROV** 16 ◄ 1968	17	18
SH 99	**WPG** 20 1984	21	22	23	**DET** 24 1971	25
26	27	28	29	30	31	

Western Hockey League

BRUARY

						1
2	3	4	5	6	7	**All Star** 8 1983
	DET 11 1982	**BUF/TB** 12 '93 / '94	13	**WASH** 14 1978	15	
OL 04	**CLEV** 17 1978	18	19	20	**BOS** 21 2000	22
23		25	26	27	28	

MARCH

OAK 3 <TML> 1970						1
2	**HART** 3 1985	4	5	**KC/CBJ** 6 '76 / '03	7	8
9	10	11	12	**NYR** 13 1976	14	15
16	17	18	19	20	**ATL** 21 1975	22
LA 23 1994	24	25	26	27	28	29
30	31					

APRIL

	1	2	3	**OTT** 4 1993	5	
6	7	8	9	**PHIL** 10 1979	11	12
13	**CAL** 14 1999	**MON** 15 1975	16	17	18	19
0	**CAL** 21 <EDM> 1988	22	23	24	25	26
27	28	**CHI** 29 1982	30			

<EDM> Edmonton at Calgary, "Battle of Alberta" classic

MAY

				1	2	3
4	5	6	7	**NYI** 8 1982	9	10
11	12	13	14	15	16	17
18	19	20	21	22	23	**NYI** 24 <PHIL> 1980
25	26	**BUF/CHI** 27 <PHIL> '75 / '95	28	29	30	31

<PHIL> Philadelphia at Buffalo Sabres, 1975

JUNE

1	2	3	4	5	6	7
8	9	10	**NYR** 11 1994	12	13	14
15	16	17	18	19	20	21
22	23	24	25	26	27	28
29	30					

HOCKEY PLAY-BY-PLAY
Around the NHL with Jim Robson

> *I liked to do broadcasts on my own because it was a lot simpler, but nowadays the young listener would probably think it was pretty dull. Working by myself, I would pick up the PA announcements of the goals and penalties, and that would give me a chance to write them down. In some rinks I picked up the announcements off the crowd mike, but in most places (including in Vancouver) we had a direct feed from the PA. I would point 'up' so the engineer would know to pipe the PA into the broadcast.*

Media guide: *Looking like a Guess Who cover band, the Barons players may have been outplayed on the ice but they did sport that '70s style.*

Right: *Chris Oddleifson cuts around Barons defenceman Greg Smith (#5) during one of Cleveland's four visits to Vancouver.*

"Good Night (Riddance) Cleveland!"
Vancouver Canucks @ Cleveland Barons–February 17, 1978

Oh, to be back in California. At least that's what the Canucks must have thought each time they visited Cleveland, where the California Seals relocated and became the Barons in 1976. Beyond the Bay Area's obvious climatic advantages, the home team had been more hospitable there, too: the Canucks piled up a record of 21–7–1 against the Seals, compared with a paltry 2–3–1 showing against the troubled Barons. And, they'd never won in Cleveland.

On this night, Vancouver's last visit to the shores of Lake Erie, Dave Gardner broke a 2–2 tie, beating Canucks goalie Curt Ridley with only 50 seconds remaining. Sadly that Friday night, only 4,589 fans bothered to turn up. The sparseness of the crowd was magnified by the fact that the Richfield Coliseum, with room for 18,544, was the largest rink in the league. The monstrous arena, built by owner Nick Mileti of the NBA Cavaliers and WHA Crusaders, was the first to have giant colour TV screens at both ends of the rink. Their presence was not lost on Canucks centre Chris Oddleifson. When asked if he thought he'd been at fault on the play leading to Gardner's goal, Oddleifson shot back, "I didn't see the replay."

But off-ice amenities could not overcome on-ice failure. The Barons missed the playoffs — and payrolls — in both

of their two seasons, leading brothers George and Gordon Gund to feel they wouldn't be missed if they moved on. Meanwhile, the Minnesota North Stars were at the brink of extinction and in search of new owners. Believing in the Twin Cities hockey market, the Gunds doubled down. They bought the struggling Stars, merged their two teams and folded the Cleveland franchise. "It's amazing that the NHL allowed Cleveland and Minnesota to merge," says Jim Robson. "It was not fair to the other clubs. They turned two ordinary teams into a Stanley Cup contender." Ten Barons players suited up for the amalgamated team. "It's no coincidence," Jim insists, "that all of a sudden after inheriting the likes of Al MacAdam and the solid goaltending tandem of Gilles Meloche and Gary Edwards, the new-look North Stars got to the Cup finals in 1981."

Vancouver's hockey connection with Cleveland and California came full circle in 1991, when the Gunds rid themselves of the North Stars to become part-owners of the San Jose Sharks. And the Canucks kept up their winning ways in northern California, going 34–23–9 against the Sharks.

DAVE GARDNER • CENTER
BARONS

"Cleveland's Richfield Arena was a huge facility built for basketball, too. It was never a success because it was built too far out of town [25 miles from downtown]. We'd stay downtown and bus out to the rink. The rink itself was a poor place to work because the broadcasters were right in the stands. I'd look over and see the coach of Cleveland, Jack "Tex" Evans, whom I'd known for a long time — from when he played for the Canucks in the WHL." — *JR*

"I used to go to Cleveland in the 1960s with the Western League Canucks because [they] played an interlocking schedule with the American League. In 1966 the leagues had a joint meeting and announced that they were going to go independent of the NHL and sign players. The next day, the NHL announced its expansion plans for 1967 in order to cut the minor leagues off at the knees." — *JR*

CLEVELAND

PERIOD 1 2 3 OT

VAN	2	F
CLEV	3	

93

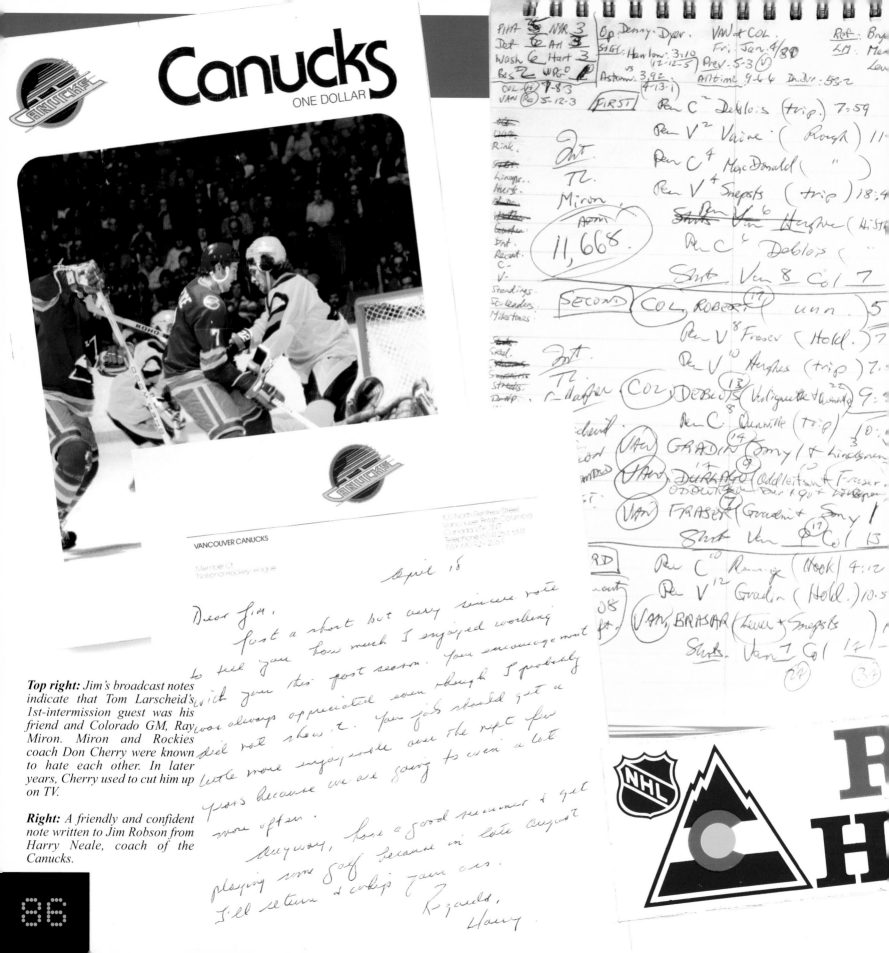

Canucks
ONE DOLLAR

VANCOUVER CANUCKS

Member Of
National Hockey League

Top right: *Jim's broadcast notes indicate that Tom Larscheid's 1st-intermission guest was his friend and Colorado GM, Ray Miron. Miron and Rockies coach Don Cherry were known to hate each other. In later years, Cherry used to cut him up on TV.*

Right: *A friendly and confident note written to Jim Robson from Harry Neale, coach of the Canucks.*

April 18

Dear Jim,

Just a short but very sincere note to tell you how much I enjoyed working with you this past season. Your encouragement was always appreciated even though I probably did not show it. Your job should get a little more enjoyable over the next few years because we are going to win a lot more often.

Anyway, have a good summer & get playing some golf because in late August I'll return & whip your ass.

Regards,
Harry

As the beleaguered Canucks entered this game against Colorado, they were a mile high in body, but not in spirit. They hadn't won on the road in over a month, and captain Don Lever was openly questioning management's recent trades. Early in the second period, when Rockies sniper Rene Robert walked in alone and trickled a puck through Canucks' goalie Glen Hanlon's pads, it looked like the start of another road loss. But on this night the Canucks rallied and held a 3–2 lead going into the third period.

Late in the third, the Rockies pulled goalie Hardy Astrom for an extra attacker, and the Canucks, clinging to their one-goal lead, were being bombarded. Robson watched as Canucks coach Harry Neale intentionally got into a beef with a fan behind the bench. "I think Harry threw a cup of ice over his shoulder and hit the fan in the face. Then the guy started to pour beer on Harry, and Harry probably insulted the fan's wife. There was a big uproar at the bench, and referee Brian Lewis had to stop the game. I remember Lewis coming over to the

bench laughing, because Harry was a smart, funny guy who had quite a rapport with the officials, having worked the lines in the IHL [International Hockey League]. Of course, Harry had stirred up the whole incident on purpose."

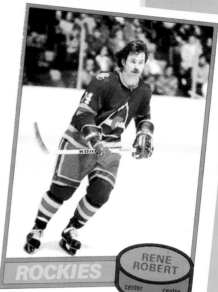

RENE ROBERT

center   centre

ROCKIES

After the game, most didn't even know about Neale's shenanigans at the bench. All people wanted to talk about was Hanlon's six game-saving stops in the third period, including four off of deflections. The 2nd-intermission radio guest, columnist Tony Gallagher of *The Province*, called the victory a "tribute to the magic of goaltender Glen Hanlon." Rockies coach Don Cherry went so far as to proclaim, "I've said it before, and I'll say it again: Glen Hanlon is the best goalie in the NHL." The envious tone of Cherry's comment was fully apparent, given that his own goalie, Astrom, was his perennial whipping boy.

In an era before timeouts and TV breaks, Neale cleverly succeeded in giving Hanlon a break. The Canucks were able to hold on to win the game — their only victory that January (they went 1–11–1).

"Like a lot of the U.S. rinks, McNichols Arena was without broadcast facilities. I'll bet the architects never even thought about it. In Canada they do, but not in the U.S. — not even in Detroit. At McNichols we sat in a little platform area, up behind the visiting team bench, in amongst the spectators. I never liked being on the players' bench side at such a low level because people are in the way and you can't see what's going on. Better to be high on the opposite side so you can see the benches." — *JR*

"The most notorious nights in Colorado with the Rockies were when they had ten-cent beer nights and they'd fill the place with college students who would all drink like crazy." — *JR*

COLORADO

OCKY
OCKEY

PERIOD 1 2 3 OT

VAN 4
COL 2   F   87

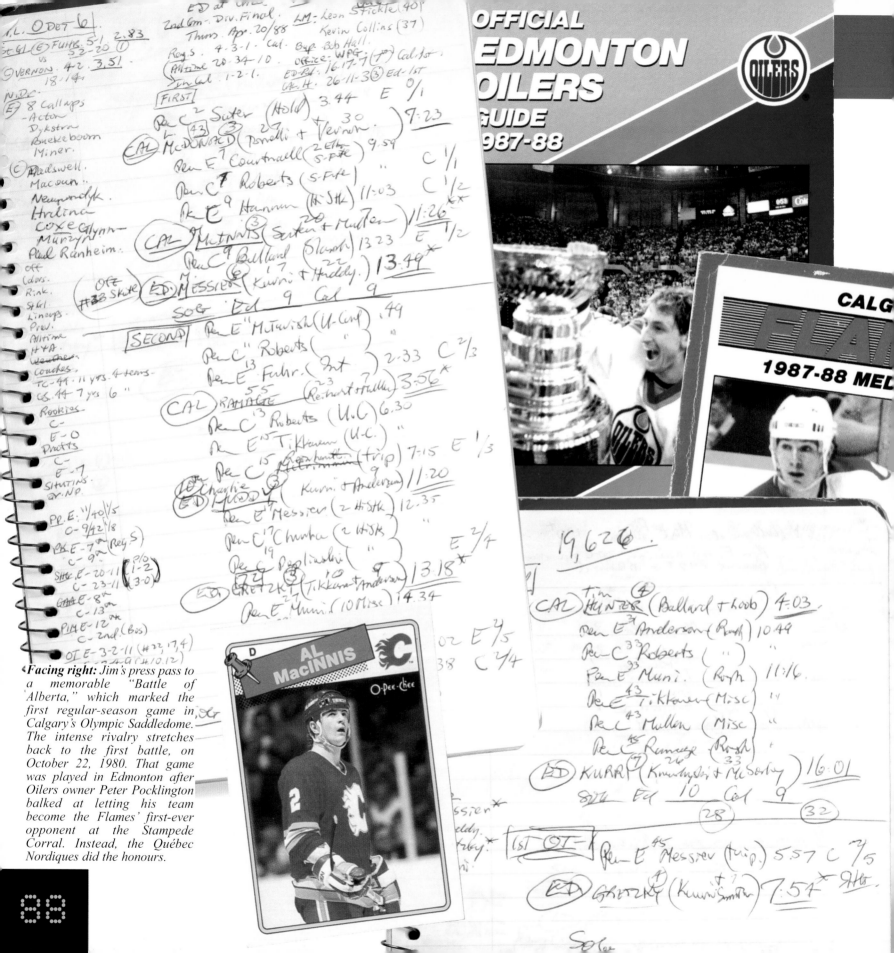

Facing right: *Jim's press pass to a memorable "Battle of Alberta," which marked the first regular-season game in Calgary's Olympic Saddledome. The intense rivalry stretches back to the first battle, on October 22, 1980. That game was played in Edmonton after Oilers owner Peter Pocklington balked at letting his team become the Flames' first-ever opponent at the Stampede Corral. Instead, the Québec Nordiques did the honours.*

OFFICIAL EDMONTON OILERS GUIDE 1987-88

CALGARY FLAMES 1987-88 MEDIA

AL MacINNIS

Gretzky Ends a Classic 'Battle of Alberta' in Overtime
Edmonton Oilers @ Calgary Flames–April 20, 1988

It's a unique streak: Every spring from 1983 through 1990 an Alberta team — the Calgary Flames or Edmonton Oilers — reached the Stanley Cup finals. And they won, more often than not: Edmonton skated home with the mug five times in six tries, while the Flames avenged a 1986 loss to the Habs by winning it all in '89.

So, when the teams met in the Smythe Division final in 1988 (the fourth such battle in six years), no one could underestimate the importance of the series — least of all the Flames, who had finished first overall in the regular season but who had lost the first game — on home ice — by a 3–1 margin.

Jim was part of the TV crew, but not for Hockey Night in Canada: The Global Television Network had bought the rights to the 1988 Calgary–Edmonton series, breaking the CBC's playoff-hockey monopoly. Joining Jim were host Dave Hodge, colour commentator John Davidson and producer John Shannon. "I liked working with Dave," Jim is quick to mention. "He is very good on air and he's a very professional guy." Yet, with a western Canadian twinkle in his eye, he continues: "When you work with Dave, he runs the whole show. I remember old HNiC games back in Toronto. Mickey Redmond and I would be asked to pick the three stars with about three minutes to go in the game. We would struggle with picking

the stars while we called the game, then send the picks downstairs. Then, when the stars were announced, none of our stars made the list. So the next time they asked us to pick the stars, I said, 'The heck with it. Just let Hodge pick them.'"

On this night, Wayne Gretzky was indisputably the game's first star. Even though the Oilers twice fell behind the Flames by two goals, Gretzky pulled Edmonton even at three with a power-play goal in the second. Calgary moved back in front on a goal by tough guy Tim Hunter — remarkably, his fourth in seven playoff games that year. But with under four minutes left in regulation time, Jari Kurri caught Flames defenceman Paul Reinhart flat-footed and easily moved around him to score and force overtime.

In the extra session, when penalties are seldom called, Oilers forward Mark Messier was sent off for tripping. With the penalty winding down, Kurri passed the puck up to Gretzky, who was in full flight coming out of the defensive zone. The Great One streaked down the ice and let go a wicked slap shot from inside the face-off circle to the right of Flames goalie Mike Vernon. The puck went in the net. The Oilers went on to sweep the Flames. And two series later, the Smythe Division champs again hoisted Lord Stanley's Mug. For Jim, the 1988 Battle of Alberta ended up becoming the last non-Canuck games that he ever called.

"The Saddledome was the quietest building in hockey, even if the building was full. It was so dull partly because of the character of the Calgary fans and partly because of the building design. The unusual dipped roof had all kinds of insulation and soundproofing." — *JR*

"The only time the fans made noise was when the Oilers came to town. Then, the crowd was always right into it because there was so much rivalry and pregame hype. Alberta fans were just as enthusiastic as the Islander–Ranger fans, but they were pro their own team. Canadian fans never stooped as low as New York fans, who took pride in being vicious toward the other teams." — *JR*

"Moving to the Saddledome was good for the Flames. The old Stampede Corral rink had boards that were higher than regulation and caused a lot of rib-cage injuries." — *JR*

"I liked doing non-Canucks games, especially playoff games. From a broadcasting standpoint, the Calgary/Edmonton games added excitement because they gave me the chance to prove to a different audience that I wasn't just a 'homer' or 'the Vancouver guy.'" — *JR*

CALGARY

$5.00

E MULLEN

PERIOD 1 2 3 OT

EDM 5
CAL 4 F OT

89

(EDM leads best-of-7 Division Final, 2–0)

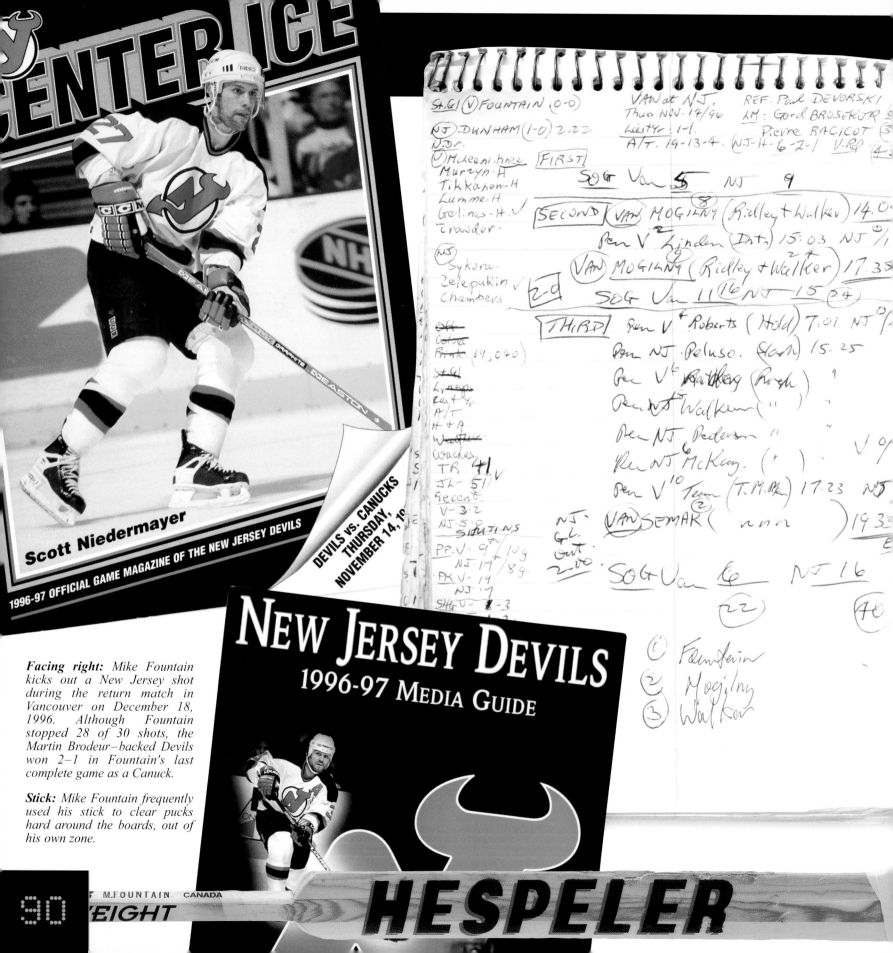

CENTER ICE

Scott Niedermayer

1996-97 OFFICIAL GAME MAGAZINE OF THE NEW JERSEY DEVILS

NEW JERSEY DEVILS
1996-97 MEDIA GUIDE

Facing right: Mike Fountain kicks out a New Jersey shot during the return match in Vancouver on December 18, 1996. Although Fountain stopped 28 of 30 shots, the Martin Brodeur–backed Devils won 2–1 in Fountain's last complete game as a Canuck.

Stick: Mike Fountain frequently used his stick to clear pucks hard around the boards, out of his own zone.

HESPELER

F M.FOUNTAIN CANADA
EIGHT

90

Fountain Showers Devils with Debut Shutout
Vancouver Canucks @ New Jersey Devils – November 14, 1996

One would think that four games in six nights during an eastern road trip might be activity enough for the Vancouver Canucks. But before the trip was half over, they would see a win, a loss, a sale, a surgery and a trade. The trip started with a 3–2 win in New York on Monday. Then Tuesday brought the news that the Griffiths family's 22-year ownership of the Canucks had come to an end as John McCaw bought out their remaining interest in Orca Bay, the Canucks' parent company. Before Wednesday's match with the Islanders, it was learned that the star of Monday's game, goalie Kirk McLean, had returned to Vancouver for arthroscopic surgery after re-injuring his knee against the Rangers. Mike Fountain was called up from the minors to back up the team's second-stringer, Corey Hirsch. On Long Island, the Canucks did not play physically enough, blew a lead and lost in overtime. That same day, Vancouver traded for tough guy Donald Brashear. Whew!

With little time to regain their collective breaths, the Canucks found themselves in tough the next night against the New Jersey Devils. Hirsch had had a poor outing against the Islanders, so Fountain drew the assignment. The Devils countered with their own Mike: goalie Mike Dunham, another neophyte with only one decision, a win, in his NHL career to date. Fountain started well, stopping all nine shots he faced in the first period. In the second, Alexander Mogilny scored twice and Fountain again came up big, stopping all 15 shots fired his way. New

Jersey carried the play in the third and peppered another 16 pucks at Fountain, for a game total of 40, but Fountain stopped them all. He almost scored an empty-netter in the last minute of the game, but his long shot curled just wide. Moments later, though, Canucks forward Alexander Semak did score into the empty net, the last marker of his NHL career.

The night belonged to the rookie Fountain. Even Jim was impressed: "Boy, he sure looked like he was going to be really good. He looked like a Kirk McLean. He was a good-sized kid who could really handle the puck." With his blanking of New Jersey, Fountain was the first goalie in over 11 years to earn a shutout in his first NHL start and only the 19th ever, joining the likes of Mario Lessard, Gary Simmons and Wayne Thomas (against the Canucks in 1973).

The Canucks, and Fountain, ended the whirlwind road trip getting blitzed 6–1 on Saturday night in Montreal. As Jim puts it, "the bloom went off in a hurry" for Fountain, who only played 125 more minutes in a Canucks jersey and would only win one more game in the NHL.

"Brendan Byrne Arena [now the Continental Airlines Arena] is a big barn out in a swamp, seven miles from Manhattan. You can see downtown from the arena. The rink is seldom full, and inside there's no character, partly because the Devils themselves aren't connected with a city or a town. When they won the Stanley Cup they had to have their parade in a parking lot!" — *JR*

"In the early years, the Devils had to take out about six rows of the highest-price seats and set up tables and chairs for the broadcasters. Since we were right in the stands, the odd time people would come by while I was on air and ask me to say hi to their Aunt Marion in Naramata or some such thing. It was a real nuisance." — *JR*

"In latter years, after a big beef between legendary Blues play-by-play man Dan Kelly and his Devils counterpart, Larry Hirsch, visiting radio got moved way up to a circular maintenance walkway called 'the halo.' From up there we were farther away than in any other rink, even MSG." [Hirsch, in total contrast to Jim Robson, was a real wild guy who would play to the fans around him while on-air.] — *JR*

NEW JERSEY

PERIOD 1 2 3 OT

VAN 3
NJ 0 F

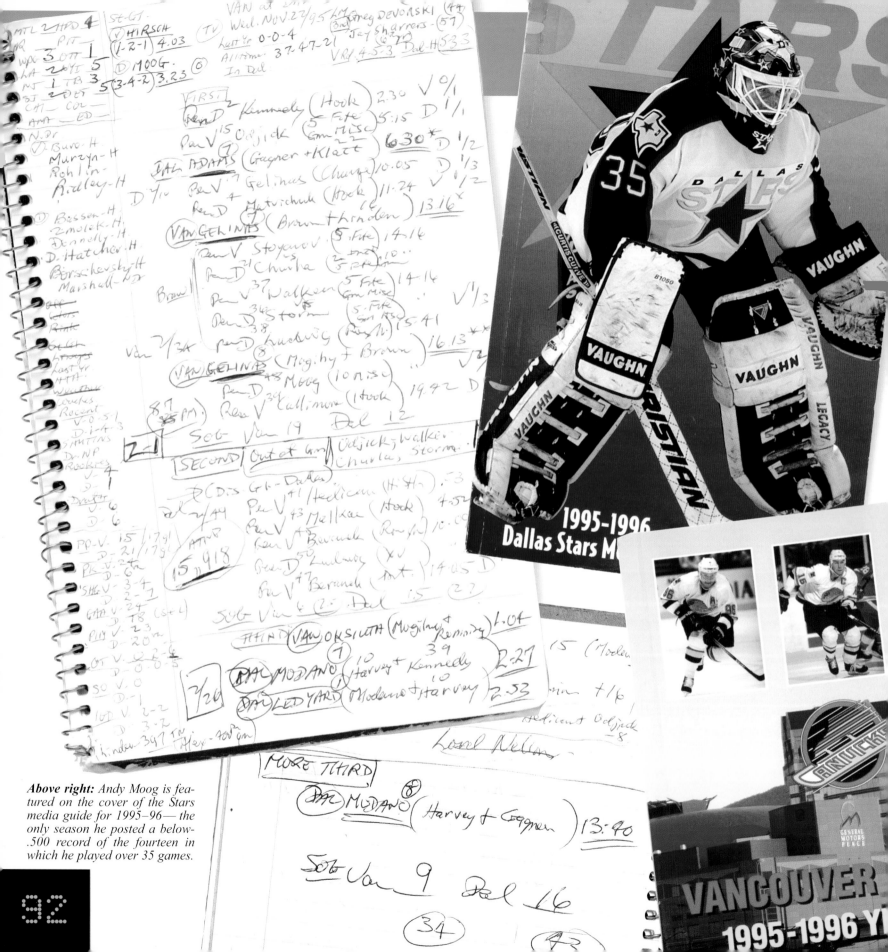

Above right: Andy Moog is featured on the cover of the Stars media guide for 1995–96 — the only season he posted a below-.500 record of the fourteen in which he played over 35 games.

1995-1996
Dallas Stars M

VANCOUVER
1995-1996 Y

November 22 is a date that is inextricably linked with the city of Dallas. On that day in 1963, President John F. Kennedy was assassinated in the city's downtown. Jim shudders when he thinks back about the significance of the date and place. "Reunion Arena is right downtown," he begins. "We stayed at a hotel right beside the arena, so you just walked out of the hotel, across a parklike area and into the arena. If you had a room on the opposite side of the hotel, you looked right down on the spot where President Kennedy was assassinated. The Book Depository building is across the highway from the hotel. Every time I saw that spot I thought how depressing it was that someone pulled off that shooting."

Like everyone of Jim's generation, he remembers vividly where he was on that fateful day in 1963. "I'll always remember where I was when JFK was shot. I heard the news on the radio in front of Holy Rosary Cathedral in Vancouver. I was on my way to the B.C. Lions' office on Seymour Street, at Dunsmuir, to do my daily radio football show with the coach, Dave Skrien." And while those distant times remain clear as yesterday, the game at hand provided plenty of drama to keep Jim in the present.

The first period served to renew persistent hostilities from the 1994 Western Conference semifinal series

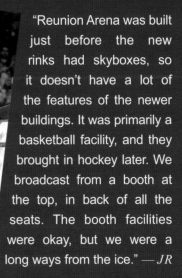

between the two teams. Four players — Gino Odjick, Scott Walker, Jim Storm and Shane Churla (Pavel Bure's number-one enemy) — were tossed from the game. Ex-Canuck Greg Adams had opened the scoring for the home side prior to the brawl, but a pair by Martin Gelinas and an early third-period goal by Roman Oksiuta put the Canucks up 3–1. From there, Stars forward Mike Modano took over. Having shaken off the rust after missing four games due to a strained abdominal muscle, Modano potted two goals and an assist in the third to steal the victory.

Modano's heroics would have been meaningless, however, had it not been for the spirited netminding of Dallas's Andy Moog, who stopped 31 of 34 shots and even drew a 10-minute misconduct for protesting Gelinas's second goal. While the Canucks' Corey Hirsch was the busier of the two goalies, his positioning and ability to provide the timely save were not as good as the veteran Moog's.

"Reunion Arena was built just before the new rinks had skyboxes, so it doesn't have a lot of the features of the newer buildings. It was primarily a basketball facility, and they brought in hockey later. We broadcast from a booth at the top, in back of all the seats. The booth facilities were okay, but we were a long ways from the ice." — *JR*

"In Dallas, we always had poor technical operators who didn't know hockey. For instance, the operators never knew when to bring up the public-address announcements in the broadcast. Despite that, for years there was always one thing good in Dallas: the management. Bob Gainey, Ken Hitchcock and Rick Wilson were all very co-operative. I'd be walking in the arena by the dressing rooms. Hitchcock's office was across the hall and he'd have the door open and call me in. He'd tell me about his lineup changes and the power-play units he was going to play. He trusted me not to run across the hall and be a spy." — *JR*

DALLAS

VAN 3
DAL 4 F

101

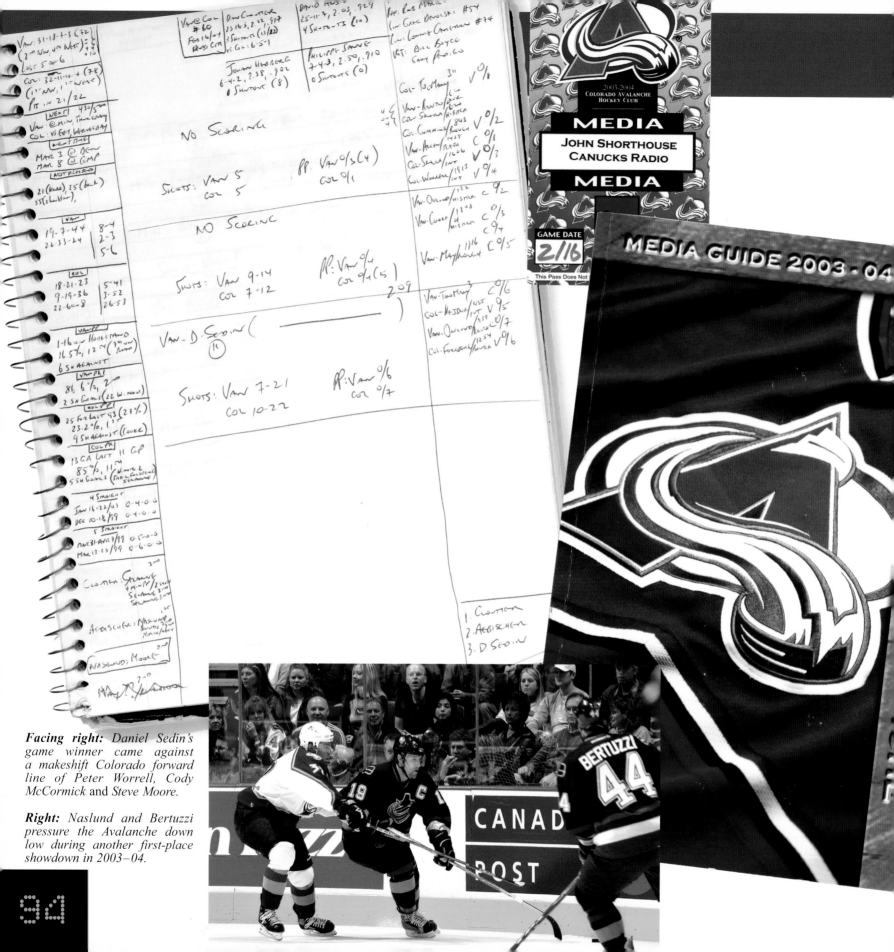

Facing right: Daniel Sedin's game winner came against a makeshift Colorado forward line of Peter Worrell, Cody McCormick and Steve Moore.

Right: Naslund and Bertuzzi pressure the Avalanche down low during another first-place showdown in 2003–04.

Coming off the All-Star break, the Canucks dropped three in a row at home and were in danger of losing their race with the Colorado Avalanche for the Northwest Division title. They took to the road for their next three games — beginning in Denver, where the Avs had lost only 1 of their past 22 games in regulation time.

The game between the two highly skilled teams had all the makings of a classic. Heading into the last minute of the second period, it was still scoreless. Then the tenor of the rivalry was changed — perhaps forever.

Naslund was out of the game, and the Canucks would retaliate in a subsequent match. The way that their actions played out, both on and off the ice, was to prove regrettable for the participants. John comments: "I find it unfortunate that probably my two most famous calls are McSorley [slashing the Canucks' Donald Brashear in 1999] and Bertuzzi [assaulting Moore in

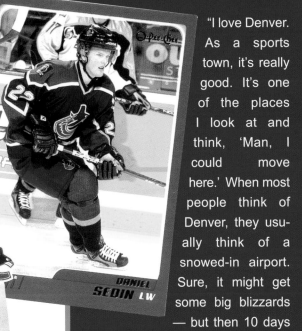

DANIEL SEDIN LW

Looking back on Avalanche forward Steve Moore's hit on Canucks captain Markus Naslund, John says, "It probably didn't get the scrutiny it deserved at the time because there was no lead-up to it. It just happened so quickly. I remember the puck went up through centre ice with Naslund chasing it and Moore chasing it. Moore veered off a bit to get a piece of Naslund — a standard hockey collision. . . . Our reaction to it wasn't, 'Oh, was that ever dirty'; it was more like, 'Man, Markus was in a vulnerable position, and Moore maybe took advantage of him a little bit, and isn't it too bad that Markus got hurt."

March 2004]. They are certainly my two most replayed calls across North America. But I'd much prefer it to be a Stanley Cup–winning goal!"

On this night, the Canucks maintained their composure. John says, "There wasn't going to be retribution because the stakes were so high and [the score] was so tight." Vancouver's restraint was rewarded early in the final frame when Daniel Sedin, skating with his brother Henrik and Todd Bertuzzi, scored the game's lone goal. The win ignited an impressive 12–6–3–2 finish to the season for the Canucks, enough to edge the Avalanche out of first place by one point. In so doing, Vancouver broke the Colorado franchise's nine-year reign as regular-season division winner.

"I love Denver. As a sports town, it's really good. It's one of the places I look at and think, 'Man, I could move here.' When most people think of Denver, they usually think of a snowed-in airport. Sure, it might get some big blizzards — but then 10 days of sunshine will follow." — JS

"I'm always amazed by how much the altitude affects me in the 'Mile-High City.' I remember on a few occasions during the 2002 playoffs there, I got light-headed during some of the more frantic play-by-play calls. I can only imagine what it's like for the players, who actually are doing physical activity!" — JS

"One promotional thing that the Avalanche organization does is to name streets around the Pepsi Center after their players. There's a Patrick Roy Street and a Rob Blake Street. I'm not exactly sure whether it works on a rotational basis, or if they have a bunch of different streets to name." — JS

COLORADO

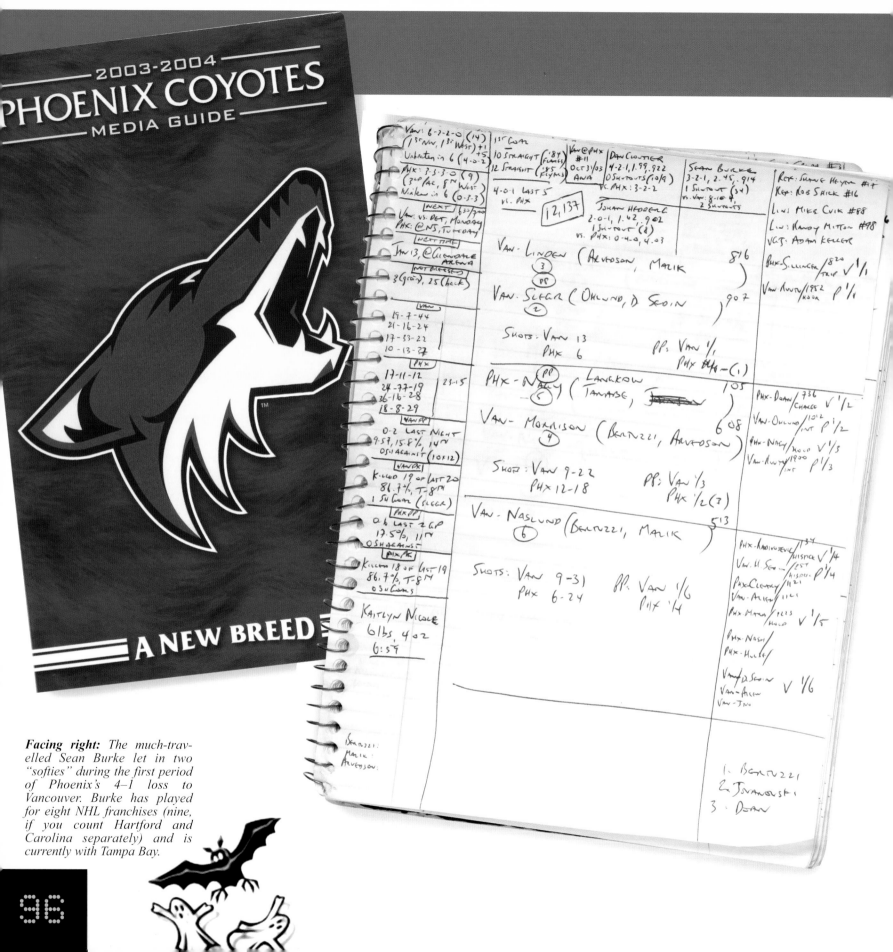

Facing right: The much-travelled Sean Burke let in two "softies" during the first period of Phoenix's 4–1 loss to Vancouver. Burke has played for eight NHL franchises (nine, if you count Hartford and Carolina separately) and is currently with Tampa Bay.

Touching down in the desert, the Canucks (unbeaten in six, 4–0–2) were thrilled to face the flagging Coyotes (winless in six, 0–3–3). But it wasn't just the fact that the teams were going in opposite directions that made the Canucks happy, explains John. "Phoenix is the trip everyone looks forward to, because quite often the schedule-maker gives the visiting team a couple of days off around their game there." Naturally, the players (and coaches!) keep their fingers crossed that the team is "going well" during their Phoenix visit so they get some time off rather than "punishment practice." John acknowledges that "some fans roll their eyes thinking that the last thing millionaire players need is a day off." But he finishes his thought by putting the matter into perspective, "The season is a grind, and just hanging out in the sunshine is a nice way for the players to bond."

It was important for the Canucks not to look past this Hallowe'en night encounter with the struggling desert dogs — if, that is, they hoped to relax during their two days off before they returned home to host Detroit on November 3. One sure-fire way to stay focused on the game at hand is to get off to a good start and score the first goal. Indeed, the secret to Vancouver's early-season success had been exactly that: They had opened the scoring in each of their first 10 games.

Thinking back on the start of the 2003–04 season, John says, "The

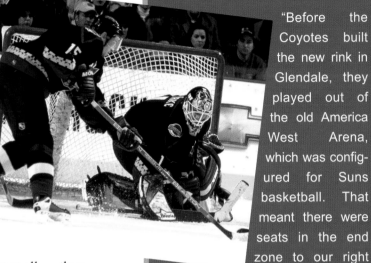

Canucks had the Midas touch there for a while. People started to talk about the fact that the Canucks were scoring first in all their games. I don't think the team cared about that at all — they just want to win — but if you look at the NHL statistically, scoring first certainly helps a team's cause." Against Phoenix, Trevor Linden found the back of the net to push the streak to 11 games — which tied the NHL record for scoring first in the most consecutive games from the start of a season.

The Canucks, as the probabilities suggest, went on to win the game 4–1 — and earn some R&R — in front of a ghoulish crowd of 12,137. "I think the jury's out regarding hockey catching on in Phoenix," John says of the modest attendance figure. "The Coyotes' new home in Glendale is one of those situations where they put a rink somewhere and are hoping that things sprout up around it. It's a bit of a risky proposition when you're talking about hockey in a non-hockey market. But still I think the chances of hockey succeeding in Phoenix are better than in places like Carolina, Nashville or even the Floridian teams. I give Phoenix a bit more of a fighting chance."

"Before the Coyotes built the new rink in Glendale, they played out of the old America West Arena, which was configured for Suns basketball. That meant there were seats in the end zone to our right where fans couldn't see the ice from probably the top of the circles in, if not the blue line in, because the seats hung over the playing surface. The views were completely obstructed. Another oddity there was that the visiting team's backup goalie had to sit by himself in the end zone to our left because the visiting bench was too small." — JS

"I didn't mind the old Phoenix rink because we broadcast from very low, right behind the benches. A location like that — close to the ice, around Row 20 on the players' bench side — is my preferred broadcast location. If a player gets hurt I can do a quick check to see how many guys are on the bench and discern if someone is missing by the jersey numbers." — JS

PHOENIX

PERIOD 1 2 3 OT

VAN 4
PHO 1 F

97

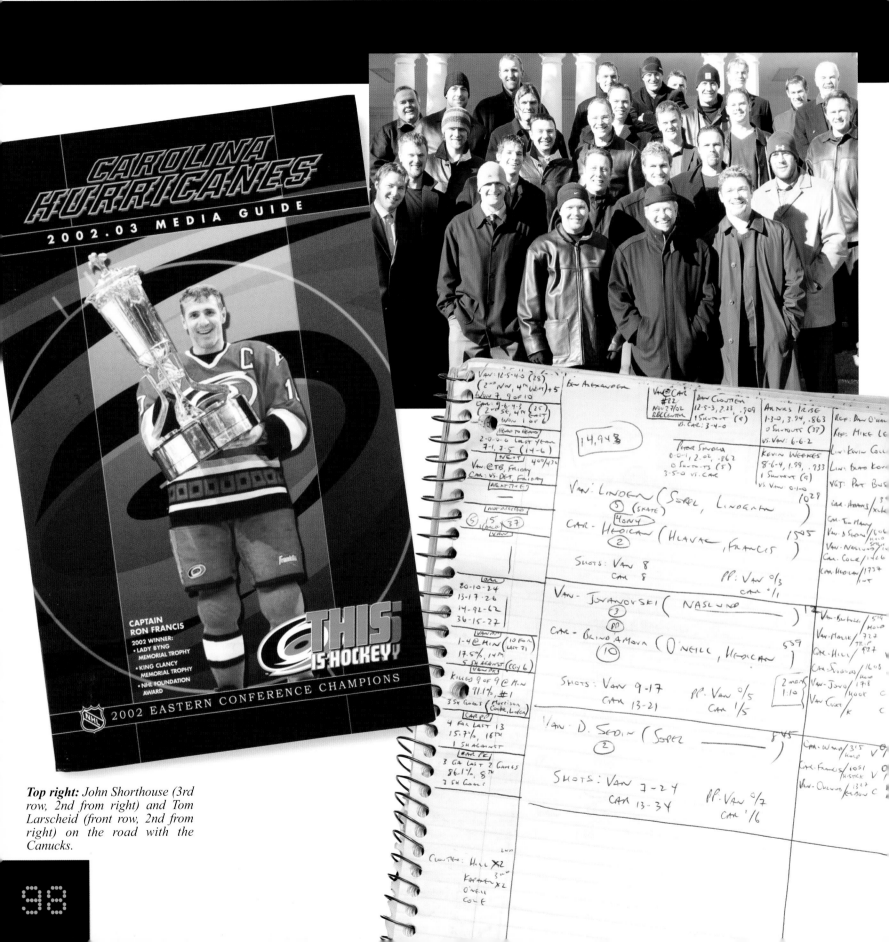

Top right: *John Shorthouse (3rd row, 2nd from right) and Tom Larscheid (front row, 2nd from right) on the road with the Canucks.*

Hurricane Watch: Canucks Get Eight Straight
Vancouver Canucks @ Carolina Hurricanes–November 27, 2002

With the pregame show from Carolina set to begin at 3:30 p.m. Pacific time, Canucks radio voice John Shorthouse jested to a reporter, "All we need now is some fog around the Cape Horn interchange." While radio ratings may have been foremost in John's mind, the Canucks — who had won their previous seven games to tie the club record set in February 1989 — had their sights firmly set on rewriting the record book.

Though his team was outshot 34–24, Canucks goalie Dan Cloutier turned in another terrific performance and Vancouver never trailed in the contest. Goals by Trevor Linden and Ed Jovanovski offset a fine game by an ex-Canuck, smooth-skating defenceman Bret Hedican, who registered a goal and an assist against his old team. But Daniel Sedin's marker near the midway point of the third period gave the Canucks a 3–2 victory along with an eight-game winning streak — a new high-water mark for the franchise.

The streak would eventually extend to 10 games, and Cloutier was deservingly named the NHL's player of the

month for November. Just thinking back to that time gets John's heart pumping. "It was a hell of a road trip when you look at it. The Canucks began the trip already sporting a six-game win streak. Then they beat Minnesota, Carolina, Tampa and Florida, before finally losing a really tough one against the Islanders. Nonetheless, the team bounced right back with a huge OT win against New Jersey, winning five out of six on the road trip. We don't see many six-game road trips anymore, so winning five out of six made for a huge trip!"

During John's tenure with the Canucks, he considers the run of 10 wins in a row "the neatest time aside from winning the playoff series [over St. Louis in 2003]." And while the streak could easily have been longer, he recalls the sentiment of the players at the time: "It was a source of pride for sure. Players know how hard it is through the course of the year to win night after night."

"The Hurricanes play in Raleigh because the state built them a building and gave them the keys. After all 18,000 seats were put in, they had to be replaced because they were the wrong shade of red for the building's other main tenant — and bigger crowd draw — the NCAA's North Carolina State Wolfpack basketball team. No question about it, though: it's a very red building." —*JS*

"Finding the shots on goal in some rinks, like Carolina, can be a challenge if they're not on the big clock. With the NHL's real-time scoring now, I could get shots off the Internet but usually I don't have enough room for my laptop. It's funny, listeners assume we have this great production company but it's really just me and Tom and the engineer. There's no stats person; we're kinda left to our own devices." —*JS*

"The Carolina radio guy, Chuck Kaiton, followed the team from Hartford and has been around forever. Chuck's been president of the NHL Broadcasters' Association since 1986. The association's big claim to fame is that members vote on the league's annual award for coach of the year." —*JS*

CAROLINA

PERIOD 1 2 3 OT

VAN 3
CAR 2   F   99

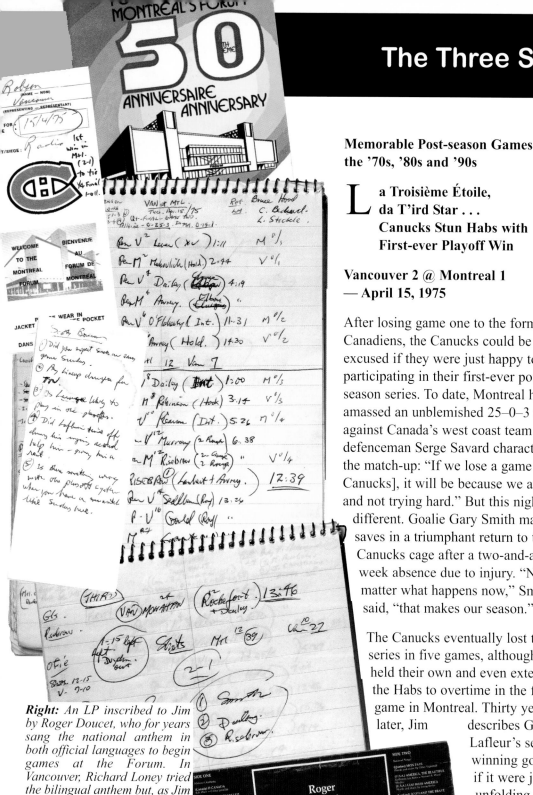

FOWARDS - cont'd

- NYSTROM – cuts in well at blue
  - crosses over to hit
  - sometimes plays lazy - let him sleep

9 – GILLIES – likes to position himself in deep slot
  - often shoots high
  - can get frustrated easily

91 – GORING – fla...

5

OFFENSIVELY

(1) Be sure to get past POTVIN at the point for 2 or 1's.
(2) Wings move into middle in nuetral zone if covered - get behind
(3) Bother SMITH - look for rebounds
(4) Can go wide around some of their defensemen

DEFENSIVELY

(1) ALERT FORECHECKING
  - look for reverses
  - lock center for sure
  - defense gets disorganized if pattern breaks down

• (2) FINISH EVERY CHECK all over ice
  - especially at blue
  - no second plays especially TROTTIER line
(3) PERSISTENT 3 on 3 especially BOSSY
(4) CLOSE POINT COVERAGE ON POTVIN
(5) TRY TO HOLD UP WINGERS to help our defense
  - especially TONELLI, NYSTROM, GILLIES
(6) WIDE WINGERS belong to defensemen
  (much quicker than CHICAGO wingers)

WE WILL WIN THE STANLEY CUP if each of us outworks his opponent eve...

Memorable Post-season Games from the '70s, '80s and '90s

La Troisième Étoile, da T'ird Star . . .
Canucks Stun Habs with First-ever Playoff Win

Vancouver 2 @ Montreal 1 — April 15, 1975

After losing game one to the formidable Canadiens, the Canucks could be excused if they were just happy to be participating in their first-ever post-season series. To date, Montreal had amassed an unblemished 25–0–3 record against Canada's west coast team. Habs defenceman Serge Savard characterized the match-up: "If we lose a game [to the Canucks], it will be because we are lazy and not trying hard." But this night was different. Goalie Gary Smith made 38 saves in a triumphant return to the Canucks cage after a two-and-a-half-week absence due to injury. "No matter what happens now," Smith said, "that makes our season."

The Canucks eventually lost the series in five games, although they held their own and even extended the Habs to overtime in the final game in Montreal. Thirty years later, Jim describes Guy Lafleur's series-winning goal as if it were just unfolding in front of him, "Lafleur threw the puck out of the corner, and before Smith could get to it, Dennis Kearns turned to try and knock it out of the air, but it hit his stick and went right by Gary Smith and into the goal. Smith just skated right off the ice, the series was over and he didn't want to hang around."

Right: An LP inscribed to Jim by Roger Doucet, who for years sang the national anthem in both official languages to begin games at the Forum. In Vancouver, Richard Loney tried the bilingual anthem but, as Jim recounts, "The Canucks asked him to stop because the fans continuously booed it on national TV. That was embarrassing."

The Second Star . . .
Mike Bossy Too Much for First-time Finalists

Vancouver Canucks 5 @ New York Islanders 6 (OT) — May 8, 1982

Jim's note next to Mike Bossy's hat-trick goal, which won game one of the 1982 finals in overtime, tells part of the

"Playoff Fever"

story: "[Bossy] stole Snepsts' pass for Minor and put his shot in off the goal post." Despite the Islanders' sweep, the rest of the story is that Canuck fans loved their team and continued thereafter to cheer for "Haaa-rold."

The First Star . . .
Canucks Force One-game Showdown for the Cup

New York Rangers 1 @ Vancouver Canucks 4 — June 11, 1994

In what remains the franchise's finest hour, the Canucks staved off playoff elimination for the fifth time in their magical 1994 run and knotted the finals at three games apiece. After calling more than 2,000 Canucks games, game six of the 1994 finals also saw Jim at his peak, as he turned in a call for the ages: "*. . . Messier hit [Linden] when he was down the second time, and Sergio Momesso is really upset at the Vancouver bench. But there is going to be that seventh game. We'll hope they can patch Linden up and get him in that one. He will play. You know he'll play. He'll play on crutches. He will play. And he'll play at Madison Square Garden on Tuesday night. The game is over! [Fireworks exploding.].*"

PERIOD 1 2 3 OT GAME OVER

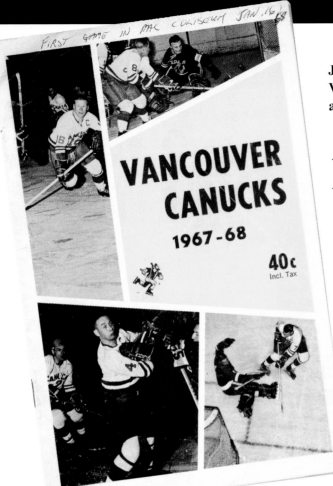

Below: *"Souvenir Edition" pamphlet promoting the new Pacific Coliseum, circa 1968.*

A note of welcome to this new exciting building

Welcome to the Pacific Coliseum. Vancouver's brand new multi-purpose exhibition and sports building is the most modern of its kind on the West Coast. Costing six million dollars it represents the very latest in design, engineering and construction. For example, the spectacular 366 foot clear roof span permits an unobstructed, column-free view for all spectators. Also, there is enough electrical power to light up a small town of 350 homes. There is almost 10 miles of pipe to make the ice for hockey, ice shows and other ice events. And everything has been considered to make everyone comfortable: from the 15,000 upholstered and semi-upholstered seats to the special grade level seating and washroom facilities for handicapped patrons. In addition, there ...l facilities for press, radio and

Jim Marks (and Makes) Vancouver Hockey History at the Pacific Coliseum . . .

First Pro Hockey Game at the Pacific Coliseum

Providence Reds 4 @ Vancouver Canucks 2 – January 16, 1968

A crowd of 12,403 showed up for opening night at Vancouver's new Pacific Coliseum. The attendance came close to the Western League record of 13,459 (set in 1963, when Los Angeles played host to San Francisco), and it was the largest gathering yet to watch a pro hockey game in Vancouver. The previous record was just under 11,000 for an Allan Cup game in 1928 at the old Denman Street Arena. The new Coliseum provided seating for 15,016, putting the Canucks in the "big leagues" after years of playing in the 5,080-seat Forum at the PNE.

Jim called the game for Vancouver radio station CKWX–AM 1130. When comparing the task of calling the WHL versus NHL games, Jim notes that "the Western League days were definitely easier because there were fewer teams, fewer commercials, and no colour guy. The players were all helmetless and easy to identify. Teams had mostly established players and might only have one or two rookies in the lineup each year, so I knew all of the players. Coaches used set lines, and because I broadcast very close to the ice in the older rinks, it was easy to spot guys even if the lines got juggled."

television personnel including a press box, a press interview room and television lounge, three dark rooms and a printing room, radio and television interview rooms, radio and television gondolas and a wire service transmitter. It is difficult to imagine construction for this ambitious building project only began in June of 1966. In the following months over 75,000 tons of earth had been excavated. By August, 1967 more than 12,000 cubic yards of concrete and 1,500 tons of reinforcing steel had been used. And by September, 1967 the 1,200 ton steel girded roof had been completed. It took a further three months to finish the inside so that the building would be complete for the January 8th opening.

L ast NHL Game at the Pacific Coliseum

Chicago Blackhawks 4 @ Vancouver Canucks 3 (OT) — May 27, 1995

Less than a year after going to game seven of the Cup finals, the Canucks were bounced from the Western Conference semifinals in four straight games by Chicago. The series was closer than the sweep suggests — the Canucks blew third-period leads in three of the games. Of interest was the fact that the last two in Vancouver both ended on overtime goals by 'Hawks defenceman Chris Chelios. So ended 27 years of pro hockey at the Coliseum — 25 of them in the NHL. During the NHL years, the Canucks accumulated a .514 winning percentage (423–400–161) on home ice, but including the Chicago series loss, they only managed to win 9 of 24 NHL playoff series played here.

Unlike all previous playoff years, Jim was no longer calling play-by-play for the playoffs. It is perhaps fitting that he watched the final game at the Coliseum from the stands — along with his son, Mike, and 15,014 other hockey fans whom he had entertained over the airwaves for all those years. Jim describes the emotion that night when

Chelios scored the winner: "There was such a down feeling in the building. Many of the longtime usherettes were crying. I couldn't believe that there was not a tribute, not even a tape

played of 'Auld Lang Syne.' No one can plan for an OT goal, but someone should have had a tape ready so the fans could bid farewell to hockey at the Coliseum. Instead, we all just filed out of there in silence."

PERIOD 1 2 3 OT   GAME OVER

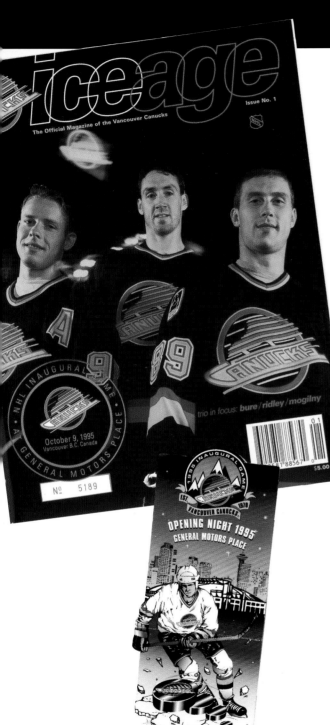

Jim Marks (and Makes) Vancouver Hockey History at General Motors Place . . .

First NHL Game at General Motors Place

Detroit Red Wings 5 @ Vancouver Canucks 3 — October 9, 1995

The Red Wings, Cup finalists the previous spring, provided the opposition for this Monday-evening opener of both the season and the new GM Place. But the event was bittersweet for Jim, whose mother passed away peacefully earlier in the day. His professional dedication carried him through his TV broadcast that day, however, as it always had, except for the passing of his mother-in-law in 1983, and for his son Rob's wedding in 1986. This inaugural game featured the answers to numerous trivia questions, most notably that Steve Yzerman scored the first goal in GM Place, while Mike Ridley scored the first Canucks goal in the new arena.

Jim's Last Play-by-Play Broadcast

Calgary Flames 5 @ Vancouver Canucks 4 — April 14, 1999

Heading into the season-ending game that would be his last-ever play-by-play broadcast, Jim admits, "I knew it was my last game, but didn't tell anyone." On the night when the Canucks' Mark Messier earned his 1,050th career assist, surpassing Gordie Howe, Calgary's Cory Stillman scored the winner with only four seconds left in the game, an appropriate end to the Vancouver franchise's worst season since 1972–73.

Over the years, hockey fans had come to respect and enjoy Jim's upbeat but balanced on-air manner, despite the frequently disappointing on-ice product. After returning from a commercial break on this night, Robson was in vintage form for one final farewell: *"The season is over for the Vancouver Canucks . . . [Banter with colour man Ryan Walter]. Okay, Ryan, very good to work with you this hockey season. Calgary finished the Canucks' season with* a 5–4 decision here on a last-minute goal. But there were some ups in this season, and there's an old saying that it's the downs in life that make the ups in life, and the ups will be on the way. That's it here; from this part of the crew at GM Place . . . [Host Perry Solkowski then closed VTV's television coverage.]."

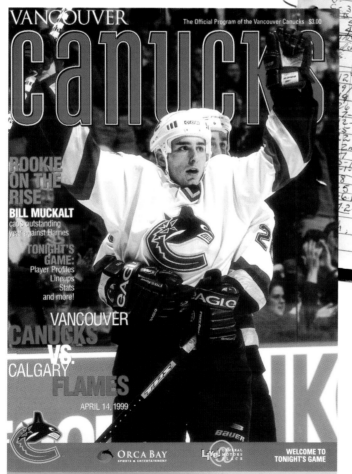

"The broadcast booth at GM Place is at the 400 level, which technically doesn't exist at GM Place. The press box is on the 500 level and then you go down a flight of stairs to get to the gondola that hangs down below, low towards the ice. For some reason they put home radio inside the blue line, as opposed to at centre ice, but you get used to it. We're pretty close to the action — we're lucky."—JS

PERIOD 1 2 3 OT GAME OVER

Author Acknowledgements

This book could not have been possible without Jim Robson's support, or his keen interest and active involvement throughout. Therefore, I am forever indebted to Jim for his support, interest, and involvement in our project. I feel humbled to be the person that Jim placed his trust in to relive and retell the many memorable nights in this book . . . as well as the ones that didn't make it in! I am especially grateful to Jim and his wife, Bea, for welcoming me into their home time and again.

Likewise, John Shorthouse believed in this project from day one and played an integral role in adding momentum and substance to it. John went out of his way to help keep me moving forward at a time in his life when there were many more pressing distractions. I feel lucky to now count Jim and John as friends; both are kind and generous people with whom I enjoy spending time.

This book came about as an offshoot of another "work-in-progress," started several years ago. On that project I had the good fortune to learn from and be assisted by terrific people. While some of them may not have contributed directly to this work, the patience they showed me and the encouragement they provided while I was learning the publishing ropes were invaluable. So to Cesare Maniago, Benny Ercolani, Tyler Wolosewich, Michael Warek, Reid Mitchell and especially to Dan Diamond, my sincere thanks. Thanks also to my friend Matthew Millward and his family for my home away from home in Toronto over those years.

The person who has worked with me the longest on my hockey research is Adrienne Painter. It is such a pleasure to work with someone who so perfectly translates what's in my head to the printed page — only better. Were it not for Adrienne generating countless "mock-ups" of layouts to pitch people over the years, this book would not have come to be. For your talent, tolerance, and tenacity, my sincere thanks, Ade.

The research and writing of this book was made much easier thanks to the terrific foundation laid over the years by the work of Dan Diamond and Associates and by members of the Society for International Hockey Research. Specifically, the *NHL Official Guide and Record Book, Total Hockey* (Second Edition) and *Total NHL* (2004 Edition) are great resources. The tattered pages of my copies provide evidence of the importance these references had to the production of this book.

My research and storylines were greatly assisted by the daily written record provided by Canuck beat writers and newspaper columnists over the years. In particular I am grateful for the earlier work by Clancy Loranger, Tom Watt, Arv Olson, Tony Gallagher, James Lawton, Mike Beamish, Lowell Ullrich, Elliott Pap, Jim Jamieson, Iain MacIntyre, Archie McDonald, Terry Bell, Jack Keating, Gary Mason, Ben Kuzma and Brad Ziemer.

I wish to thank the following people for their invaluable assistance in helping me produce and distribute this book: Jo Blackmore(*www.granvilleislandpublishing.com*), Lloyd Davis, Gary Beale, Andrew Castell, Craig Campbell, Heidi Nucklaus, Rebecca Davies, Neall Calvert, Glen Clark, John Olson, Jennifer Smith, Graham Wall, Eric Zweig, Filomena Nalewajek, Ron Kuehl and my terrific assistant, Kim Lee. My thanks also to Orca Bay Sports and Entertainment for their co-operation with this book, and in particular to Paul Dal Monte, Norm Jewison and Jason Steensma.

I would also like to thank the following people for lending their names, contacts and support to this project from the outset: Don Prior, Michael Korenberg, Arthur Griffiths, Greg Douglas, Bob Addison, Trevor Linden, Gerry Sillers, Dan Russell, Harry Neale and Ron McLean. Your swift responses to my many requests are both a testament to your generosity and, I know, a show of the respect you each have for Jim.

Most importantly, a special word of appreciation to my wonderful wife, Sarah, who again put her dreams on hold while I pursued mine. Thank you for always supporting me.

Photography and Memorabilia Credits

The majority of the artifacts found in this book were photographed from the personal collections of Jim Robson, John Shorthouse, Jason Farris and Canucks historian Andrew Castell.

The author gratefully acknowledges the people and organizations that provided the balance of the photos and memorabilia:

Hockey Hall of Fame: Dave Sandford: 75, 97; HHoF archives: 16 (fact book), 22 (magazine), 36 (magazine), 58 (ticket), 60 (magazine), 74 (magazine), 84 (ticket), 93 (top);

Trevor Linden: 78 (puck), 101 (trophy);

Orca Bay Sports & Entertainment: Bill Cunningham: *vi* (top), 10, 50 (bottom), 67, 84 (b/w photo), 109; Jeff Vinnick: 1 (right), 15, 62, 69, 77, 79, 94; Jack Murray: 13, 37 (top), 61; Norm Jewison: 35; Ralph "Railbird" Bower: 46; Kent Kallberg: 91; Canucks archives: *iii* (left), *viii*/1 (middle), 1 (bottom), *viii* (left), 20, 82 (top);

St. Petersburg Times Forum: 64, 65 (2);

Jeff Vinnick: *iii* (right), 14 (bottom), 68 (top and bottom), 82 (bottom), 98;

Frank J. Zamboni & Co., Inc.: 37.

All memorabilia was photographed by Gary Beale, B-Plus Studios Ltd.

Front cover photo: *Jim Robson in his perch above Section 25 of the "greens" at the Pacific Coliseum in Vancouver during the Canucks' first NHL season, 1970–71. The photo is reproduced from Jim Robson's personal collection and is believed to have been taken by Bill Cunningham.*

ZAMBONI and the configuration of the Zamboni® ice resurfacing machine are registered trademarks of Frank J. Zamboni & Co., Inc.

From Jim's Broadcasting Peers

Most people think of music when referring to the "soundtrack of their life," but for me it's the voice of Jim Robson calling Canucks games.

Whether describing action around "the north goal to my right at the Pacific Coliseum," giving a "special hello to hospital patients" during a play stoppage at the Boston Garden, or being heard above the unmistakable roar at Chicago Stadium — no matter where the location, listening to Robson was always the highlight of my day.

Not only is Robson the absolute all-time best at his craft, but I can honestly tell you that without his influence, my *Sportstalk* show wouldn't exist.

— Dan Russell, host of Canada's longest-running sports talk program

From "Shut-ins"

Sports mean a great deal to those of us without sight, and we especially enjoy your commentary. Your descriptions of all the games give us a clear and vivid picture. The plays become alive and we can see all the plays on the rink. We are true fans. We would give up television any day to listen to you describe our local team. Foster Hewitt has always been considered one of the favourite broadcasters in Canada, but I wonder if you realize that here in B.C. you are held in high honour and we feel you are equally great.

I have always had a keen interest in hockey. I have never played but went to many games when I could see. Now I rarely miss a broadcast, especially knowing that it would be Jim Robson doing the commentating.

[I] appreciate your tremendous understanding of the needs of the shut-ins and the blind themselves. . . . Yours is a job well done.

— 1971 letter to Jim from A.J. "Tony" Mazzucco, New Westminster, B.C.

Award of Appreciation
~ Jim Robson ~
"Voice of the Vancouver Canucks"
For never failing to remember us "Shut-ins"
~ from the boys at Mountain Institution ~

September 21, 1992

Mr. Jim Robson
The Hockey Hall of Fame
Induction Dinner
c/o The Westin Hotel
Toronto, Ontario

Dear Jim:

Tonight is one night where no one will need to call the play-by-play! The word will get out anyhow that you have rightfully been inducted into The Hockey Hall of Fame.

I have always enjoyed my visits with you, Jim, and want to take this opportunity on behalf of all of the active players in the N.H.L. to thank you for the great service you have provided to our game.

I look forward to seeing you again soon, and I sincerely hope that this evening will be a memorable one for you and your family.

Your Friend,

Wayne

Wayne Gretzky

11755 Wilshire Blvd., Suite 850, Los Angeles, California 90025

From Hockey Fans Everywhere

Like many west coast hockey fans, I have wonderful childhood memories of lying in bed at night listening to Canucks games — and Jim Robson was the key ingredient. I just closed my eyes and he would paint the picture for me. In the spring of 1982, my Little League baseball team was sitting in its dugout, listening to game one of the Stanley Cup finals on a small transistor radio, and no one wanted to go up to bat because the game was in overtime. Our team was so disinterested in the ballgame at hand, just mesmerized by Robson's play-by-play.

Robson held our attention because he had the ability to raise the level of excitement and intensity in his broadcast at key times in a game, yet maintain poise, control and accuracy in his voice. Like the superstars on the ice, Robson seemed to be able to slow the game down in his head. It was as if Robson, like Gretzky, could see the play developing before it happened and already be in a position to make the perfect call. Thanks, Mr. Robson, for being a trusted companion to me and to hockey fans everywhere.

— Jim Wall, Vancouver, B.C.

Hello again to all hockey fans:

Although I retired from broadcasting at the end of the 1998–99 season, like you, I remain a big fan of the game that was so good to me — hockey. As a youngster growing up in western Canada listening to Foster Hewitt, and then Danny Gallivan, I never thought I would get the opportunity to broadcast National Hockey League games. When the chance came along, I never thought I'd end up being honoured by the Hall of Fame just for doing my job; and I certainly never thought I'd get the chance to help produce a book like this, which lets me relive so many of my memorable nights. I'm glad I kept my game notes over the years, and some of the mementos that adorn the pages of this book. I'm pleased to know that this book preserves these items from the games I called, so they are recorded for posterity. Mostly I hope the book brings back happy memories of exciting moments for hockey fans everywhere.

During all of those nights that I called, and you listened to, play-by-play of the game's great players, I had the pleasure of working with some outstanding professionals and great people in broadcasting. I was always proud to be the voice of the Vancouver Canucks since their inception in the NHL, and in the minor leagues before that. My retirement was made much easier knowing that first Jim Hughson and now John Shorthouse carried on where I left off. Both are terrific broadcasters, and whether on TV or radio, their audience is getting the best in the business.

I now spend my days enjoying time with my family and exploring this great province and country with my wife, Bea. I have always been lucky because a loyal sports wife is a very special person. I have been lucky that my career and this book always had Bea's full support and encouragement. We are both happy that the memories and excitement can be enjoyed anew by our children Jennifer, Rob, Mike and Stephani . . . without me having to go on an eleven-day, seven-game eastern road trip!

I hope that whenever you open *Hockey Play-by-Play*

Right: Jim interviews Canucks coach & GM Harry Neale in the early '80s — before the advent of the postgame scrum.

it gives you another view of the great game of hockey in the NHL cities of today and yesteryear. As a member of the media, my figurative place in hockey is just a small one — and so was my literal place — usually in a small booth high above the ice! Really, it's the owners, the general managers, the coaches, the officials, and above all, the players who are to be celebrated. . . .

This is Jim Robson, bidding you "Good night from Vancouver."

ATND.
15,062

LA at VAN.
FRI. OCT. 9.
FIRST GAME 1970   (TV)

Ref. L. Gilmour
Lin Neil Armstrong
Malcolm Ashford

7.01:
(V) McLEAN (4)
(11-5) 2.10
vs
(T) POTVIN (3)
(9-8) 2.41
N.D

B. Pollock   TOR
G. Ray   Tues
G. Gong
Chas VARITANGO   CON
Dean WARD   P.ov

1st. Pen LA¹ Rutherford (Delay game) 7.26

        Pen LA² Hogansen (Fite. 2) 5.37

        Pen V¹ Kurtenbach (" 5) 5.37

        Pen V² Quinn + MIS (Int.) 11.23.

        Pen LA³ Marotte (Int) 15.68

            VAN   11   LA   13

(V) Murzyn H
Plausic
Steyr
Charbonneau
Carson
Antoski
Recce
(T) Fountain
Borehousky
Arreault
Lacroix
McRae
Martin
Kulashov
Cullen

FIRST
            2nd
            JP.
            RW

TOR LA

Pe V

TOR. Gi

TOR CL

SOG

SECOND
VAN LA

2nd. Pen LA⁴ Glenn (H. Stick) Bill

        Pen V³ Carrigan (Hook)

LA. LONSBERRY (

Pen LA Flett (Held) 11.57

LA. BERRY°   Fite + Rufrd

        VAN   6 (17)   LA   (25)

Off
Glen
Rink
Sdel
Lougs
Prou
Wardson
Coaches:
LOAD
ROOKES
Druitz
V. 3

2nd
JP.
RW
Marc
Hebscher

Re T

Re T

VAN ADA

SOG

3-3

3rd. Pen LA² Lonsbury (Fite) 1.41.

        Pen LA² Rutherford (Roughl)

        Pen V⁴ Parmentier (Fite 5) "

        Pen V⁵ Dodd (Rough)

VAN. WILKENS (Lundu -) :17

        Pen V⁶ (Quinn) (Hold) 4.30

LA. BERRY° (Van.) 10.04

        Pen LA⁵ Kelimin (Dirt) 15.24

            8 (25)   (37)

Shitatinals
Dr. N.P.
Upcoming

PP. V 5/15
    T 1/21
PK V 7
    T 6
SHG V 1-1
    T 4-1
GM V 4
    T 5
GF V 53
    T 47
PIM V 10
    T 5
OT V 4-1
    T 3-1
SO V 4-0
    T 3-2

R/S
T13
12
12
11
4-11
8-9
17
6
14
13
5
7
5-4-3
4-1-12
3-1
3-5

THIRD

ATND
16/50

1st OT

2ND OT

VAN

McLeon
SO 5th
35.23

HAMC 1) Aa
       2) Gr
       3) Gi

REF: BILL McCREARY

Gord Broseker
Randy Mitton
3/4 T.Gregson / S & Nor.
TORONTO: Calgary

Gartner) 7.54
(Hold.) 11.27 T 1/1
Berkevstiy + Elliott) 11.37
) 12.19
TOR 10 3-0
AVEN (Courtnall + 35) 1.34

Craven + Courtnall) 9.31
ville (Clear) 13.09 V/0
wder (Rough.) / V 1/
+ Burr) 17.57 V
Botvin (Hag) 30
Antique (Rough)
3 + Jan 8 18

Elliott (X V) 4.43
(X V) 6.24 V 1/3
me (Slash)
luck (Rough) 7.43 T 1/
(Hold.) 8.44 V 1/
35 TOR 9 27

45 Tor 7 34

Baloesch +)
Lorrelle .14
V. T
4-3

St.
V. McLEAN 4
(12-5) 2.11
NY RICHTER
(12-4) 1.84 4

N.Dr.
V. S.Murzyn
Plavsic
Siegr.
Carson
Charbonneau
ODJICK
Peca
Fountain

Olczyk
Hudson Jack
Hartman McI
Kypreos
Karpotsev

atas
Tink
St.Et.
inept
Pred
t+A.
Weather
Scratches
L'LAND.
Rookies
V.
NY.
Drafts
NY.
HUTLINS.

P/o Reg.S
PO V. 5/16 TT 3
NY. 3/16 1st
2K V. 7th 12th
NY. 1st 3.8
HG V. 1-1 14-11
NY. 1-2 20-5
4 AA V. 4th 17
NY. R nd 4
F V. 57 14
NY. 60 7-t-ft
3 NY V. 10 5th
NY. 11 11
2T V. 5-1 54-3
NY. 2-1 3-1-8
O V. 4-0 3-1
NY. 4-0 7.

3 Stars
1 Game
Hel

CR
Mike INFANTINO
+
Annette Williams
+
Alan Derbez

VAN at NY.
Tues May 31/94. LM
ST. CUP FINAL.
GAME ONE.
Reg. S. 34 NY
2-5 V

REF Terry Gregson 9.
3rd Final.
Randy Mitton 2oT
Ray Scapinello 33
S/B Bill McCreary (13th)
Kevin Collins
Office: BOSTON
P/o V. Reg. 10 2 NYR 7-2

FIRST

Pen NY 2 Wells (X V) h47 V 0/1
Pen V 2 Linden (trip) 2.26 NY 0/1
NY 3 Stars 6 LARMER (Kovalev + Leetch) 3.32 (4A)
Pen V 4 McIntyre (Rough) 8.50
Pen NY 4 Lowe (") "
Pen V 6 Craven (Slash) 10.35 NY 0/2
Pen NY Brickdoorn (But) 15.54 V 0/2
SOG Van 10 NYR 15 1-0

SECOND Pen NY 8 Messier (Hook) .20 V 0/3
Pen NY 10 Lidster (trip) 8.49 V 0/4
Pen V 8 Courtnall (But.) 13.18 NY 0/3
Pen V 10 Momesso (ButG) 16.15 NY 0/4
Pen NY 12 Brickdoorn (HiStk) 19.34 V 0/5
1-0 SOG Van 5 15 NYR 9 24

THIRD VAN Bret REDICAN (Lumme + Adams) 5.45
OT NMR Alex KOVALEV (Leetch Beukeboom) 8.29
Van RONNING 19.00
2-2 GELINAS (Ronning + Momesso.)
SOG Van 7 21 NYR 13 37

1st OT Pen V 12 Momesso 7.31
Pen NY 14 Gilbert (")
3-2 VAN Greg ADAMS (Ronning + Burr) 19.26
SOG Van 9 NYR 17

Preceding page:
1970 Los Angeles at Vancouver — Vancouver Canucks' first-ever NHL game
1994 Stanley Cup Semi-finals — Canucks eliminate Leafs in double-overtime
1994 Stanley Cup Finals game 1 — McLean stops 52 shots; Canucks win at MSG